Hidden Heart of the Cosmos

REVISED EDITION

T0047608

ECOLOGY AND JUSTICE

An Orbis Series on Integral Ecology

ADVISORY BOARD MEMBERS
Mary Evelyn Tucker
John A. Grim
Leonardo Boff
Sean McDonagh

The Orbis Series on Integral Ecology publishes books seeking to integrate an understanding of Earth's interconnected life systems with sustainable social, political, and economic systems that enhance the Earth community. Books in the series concentrate on ways to:

- reexamine human-Earth relations in light of contemporary cosmological and ecological science
- develop visions of common life marked by ecological integrity and social justice
- expand on the work of those exploring such fields as integral ecology, climate justice, Earth law, ecofeminism, and animal protection
- promote inclusive participatory strategies that enhance the struggle of Earth's poor and oppressed for ecological justice
- deepen appreciation for dialogue within and among religious traditions on issues of ecology and justice
- encourage spiritual discipline, social engagement, and the transformation of religion and society toward these ends

Viewing the present moment as a time for fresh creativity and inspired by the encyclical *Laudato Si'*, the series seeks authors who speak to ecojustice concerns and who bring into this dialogue perspectives from the Christian communities, from the world's religions, from secular and scientific circles, or from new paradigms of thought and action.

Hidden Heart of the Cosmos

Humanity and the New Story

REVISED EDITION

Brian Thomas Swimme

ORBIS BOOKS
Maryknoll, New York 10545

ORBIS BOOKS
Maryknoll, New York 10545

Fathers and Brothers
MARYKNOLL™

Founded in 1970, Orbis Books endeavors to publish works that enlighten the mind, nourish the spirit, and challenge the conscience. The publishing arm of the Maryknoll Fathers and Brothers, Orbis seeks to explore the global dimensions of the Christian faith and mission, to invite dialogue with diverse cultures and religious traditions, and to serve the cause of reconciliation and peace. The books published reflect the views of their authors and do not represent the official position of the Maryknoll Society. To learn more about Maryknoll and Orbis Books, please visit our website at www.maryknollsociety.org.

About the cover graphic: Known as Metatron's Cube, it is meant to symbolize the underlying geometric patterns found throughout the universe.

Copyright © 2019 by Brian Thomas Swimme.

This is a revised edition of The Hidden Heart of the Cosmos: Humanity and the New Story by Brian Swimme, Maryknoll, NY: Orbis Books, 1996.

Published by Orbis Books, Box 302, Maryknoll, NY 10545-0302.

All rights reserved.

No part of this publication may be reproduced or transmitted in any form or by any means, electronic or mechanical, including photocopying, recording, or any information storage or retrieval system, without prior permission in writing from the publisher.

Queries regarding rights and permissions should be addressed to: Orbis Books, P.O. Box 302, Maryknoll, NY 10545-0302.

Manufactured in the United States of America

Library of Congress Cataloging-in-Publication Data

Names: Swimme, Brian, author.
Title: Hidden heart of the cosmos : humanity and the new story / Brian Thomas
  Swimme.
Description: REVISED EDITION. | Maryknoll : Orbis Books, 2019. | Series:
  Ecology and justice, an Orbis series on integral ecology | Includes
  bibliographical references and index.
Identifiers: LCCN 2019015776 | ISBN 9781626983434 (print)
Subjects: LCSH: Astronomy—Religious aspects—Christianity. | Cosmology. |
  Apologetics.
Classification: LCC BL253 .S85 2019 | DDC 113—dc23 LC record available at
  https://lccn.loc.gov/2019015776

To my parents,
Wayne and Jeanne Swimme

Contents

Preface to the First Edition   ix

Preface to the Revised Edition   xi

Acknowledgments   xv

1. The Way of Cosmology   1

2. A Three-Hundred-Thousand-Year Lineage   7

3. The Whirling Solar System   18

4. Cosmology and Ecstasy   29

5. The Sun as the Center   32

6. Looking Down on the Milky Way   40

7. A Large-Scale View of Space and Time   50

8. The Story Came to Us   57

9. Nighttime and Cosmic Rebirth   62

10. The Place Where the Universe Began   69

11. A Multiplicity of Centers   74

12. Cosmic Desire   84

13. Universe Guidance   92

14. The Origin   98

15. All-Nourishing Abyss   105

16. Einstein's Awakening   113

17. The Center of the Cosmos   120

Index   123

Preface to the First Edition

From the beginning, humans have been pondering the ultimate nature of existence. Shamans and sages, philosophers and saints, rishis and rabbis and theologians, all in their various ways, have reflected on the deep and endlessly fascinating questions of existence. *Hidden Heart of the Cosmos* wants to join that ancient tradition by asking the same questions, but from the perspective of contemporary science. Our reflections begin with the universe as science has come to know it: a universe that began fourteen billion years ago as hot, dense plasma, that constructed trillions of galaxies and stars, and that complexified further into living beings.

The question I consider here is perhaps the most ancient of all. "Where did it all come from? Where is the heart or center of the universe? Where is that place from which everything sprang forth?" Relying on the discoveries of the modern scientific enterprise, and in particular on twentieth-century cosmology and quantum physics, we confront this perennial question not with any naive expectation that we will now answer with certitude questions that eluded our ancestors, but with the hope that we too might become just as engaged by the questions, and just as baffled and amazed by the answers.

Should speculations originating from the world of science assist humanity in meeting and overcoming the challenges that beset us here at the eve of the third millennium, we will be justified in asserting that science as a whole now enters a new phase of its journey. No longer simply the handmaid of technology, no longer simply a materialistic study of reality, science will come to be understood as a powerful pathway into the deep wisdom embedded in the universe.

Preface to the Revised Edition

Twenty-five years have passed since I wrote this slim book with its daring title, *Hidden Heart of the Cosmos*. For this new edition I have gone through the text to update the science. The one major difference is that in the 1990s the best rough estimate of the universe's age was 15 billion years. Now it's 14 billion, rounded up from 13.799 billion.

My primary aim twenty-five years ago was to share the news that mathematical cosmologists had located the birthplace of the universe. But as I reviewed the text in 2019, I was surprised to find early on a diatribe against consumerism! Why had I gone so rapidly from extolling the stunning fact of science's discovery to a strong critique of the effects of advertisements on our children?

I realize now, decades later, that an ancient cosmological ritual had captured me. In traditional cultures all around the planet and back through time, when elders present the mysteries of the universe, they require participants to undergo a purification rite. Without my knowing what I was doing, I had constructed something similar. Before plunging into a celebration of the magnificence of the cosmos, I put my readers through a brief reflection on "consumerism," an element of modern consciousness that cried out for conversion. The change I would make today would be to add on other elements, especially militarism, racism, and sexism. In my warnings to parents concerned with the effects of television on their offspring, I would include a critique that goes beyond television. We will be such a conundrum for future historians: we deluge the tender souls of our children with the repulsive violence of our computer games, and then we express shock at the ensuing slaughter in the real world.

We are living through history's greatest transition in our understanding of the universe. Our knowledge dwarfs Copernicus's announcement that Earth spins around the Sun. Many hundreds of books and documentary films have been made about the time-developmental universe, and many more will be made. But simultaneous with our need to learn the nature of our evolving cosmos is the urgent necessity of discovering how to live in alignment with the Earth and the universe. It took the genius of Thomas Berry to recognize the emergence of a qualitatively new cosmology as leading to a profound transformation of human civilization. In *Hidden Heart of the Cosmos* I offer some practices for integrating the counterintuitive nature of science's discoveries, including our relationship to the birthplace of the universe, to the omnicentric nature of the universe, and to the nonvisible, generative ground of our existence. These personal transformations of consciousness find their fulfillment in the reshaping of our cultures and societal institutions.

In 2011, Mary Evelyn Tucker and I released a multimedia project, the *Journey of the Universe* film, book, and conversations. Six years later, Mary Evelyn and John Grim mounted Massive Open Online Courses (MOOCs) from Yale/Coursera titled "Journey of the Universe: A Story for Our Times," available for free on the Internet in every country. In one of the courses, "Journey of the Universe Conversations," a comprehensive program of Earth renewal is suggested for moving from an industrial to an ecological society. Here scholars and designers discuss innovative plans for renewing our cities, our economies, our agriculture, our gender relations, our energy use, our educational systems, our racial relations, and our religious traditions.

In 2015, Pope Francis released *Laudato Si'*, the most significant, single statement of the necessity to align our civilizations with the integral ecology of our Earth Community. Its penetrating analysis, together with its comprehensive vision of how we must change, can be considered one of the first moments the Earth Community as a whole reflects upon itself from the perspective of evolutionary and ecological cosmology. *Laudato Si'* is a planetary vision of a vibrant future; the "Journey of the Universe Conversations" is an action plan for realizing this vision. These initiatives and others coming forth from the hidden heart of the cosmos are manifestations of a planet in the midst of reinventing itself.

Acknowledgments

The cosmological vision articulated in *Hidden Heart of the Cosmos* had its origin in 1982 at the Riverdale Center for Religious Research in the Bronx, founded by Thomas Berry, and was carried forward in three educational endeavors: the Institute in Culture and Creation Spirituality at Holy Names University in Oakland, founded by Matthew Fox; the Philosophy, Cosmology, and Consciousness Program at the California Institute of Integral Studies in San Francisco, inaugurated by Richard Tarnas; and the Adult Education Series at Christ the King Church, founded by Rev. Brian Thomas Joyce. Conversations with the four founders, with colleagues Mary Evelyn Tucker, John Grim, Bruce Bochte, Denise Swimme, Robert McDermott, Sean Kelly, and the students in my courses brought *Hidden Heart of the Cosmos* into its final form. I am grateful for the editorial guidance provided by Marie Cantlon, for the digital images created by our son Brian Sebastian, and for the honor of being included in the literary enterprise established by Tucker, Grim, Leonardo Boff, and Sean McDonagh in Ecology and Justice—An Orbis Series on Integral Ecology.

1

The Way of Cosmology

The really surprising thing is that the news of the birthplace of the universe has always been here. For as long as humans have been on Earth, news of the universe's birthplace has showered us day and night. We have had the truth right in front of us, yet we were unable to recognize it. News of our birthplace has been carried to us by particles of light—photons. The problem is that the photons are too dim to be seen by the unassisted human eye. Just think of how many humans since history's beginning have wandered about, immersed in news of the origin of the universe but incapable of responding to what was, quite literally, right there before them.

The entire scientific enterprise can be characterized as the development of sensitivities necessary to become more fully aware of the reality all around us. Seen from this perspective, the discovery of the birthplace of the universe is a four-million-year learning event. I say four million years because, though it's difficult to identify where we should mark the beginning of humanity, one

crucial moment in our emergence was when our ancestors began walking on two legs. On the other hand,
some anthropologists prefer the moment when our ancestors began using tools in a systematic way, around
two and a half million years ago. In either case, one has
to stop and wonder at this drama with humans wandering about, thinking, working, mating, and suffering, for
millions of years, and throughout every moment of that
long journey they being bathed by the light from the beginning of time.

Most physicists regard the discovery of the birthplace of the universe as the most significant discovery of
the twentieth century. The enormously complex task involved thousands of scientists from many countries over
hundreds of years. Only by careful and painstaking investigation of the universe—collecting data, developing
new mathematical languages, debating interpretations
—were they able to arrive at their momentous finding. In
exploring the cosmos, modern scientists have as a basic
aim discovering and making known basic truths regarding our world and our universe. Yet, the greater challenge has to do with identifying the meanings such
discoveries have for human existence.

The ideas presented in this book are rooted in the
conviction that we are in the early years of a new era of
humanity. The discovery of the universe's birthplace
and its evolution calls for our deepest reflection. Though
science's rejection of cultural and tribal traditions has
been extreme, the opportunity of our time is to integrate
science's understanding of the universe with more an

cient intuitions concerning the meaning and destiny of humanity. The promise of such work is that through such an enterprise the human species as a whole will begin to embrace a shared meaning and a coherent program of action.

One way to identify the significance of what is taking place is to say that science now enters its wisdom phase. The new cosmology is part of our contemporary exploration of the wisdom within the great discoveries of the scientific enterprise as a whole. We are challenged here with understanding the significance of the human enterprise within an evolving universe. Upon our success in meeting this challenge rests the vitality of so much of the Earth Community, including the quality of life all future children will enjoy.

In considering the discovery of the center of the cosmos, we need to bear in mind that it is different from the discovery of the Grand Canyon. If I were among the first Paleo-Indians to see the Grand Canyon and wanted to share it with a friend, I would just take her there and point out the massive red walls, the crumbling sun-baked rocks, the distant low hush of the hidden river. Though the birthplace of the universe has physical dimensions and can be, in a sense, pointed at, it is a different kind of reality than the Grand Canyon, or the African elephant, or the Sistine Chapel. After all, if the center were the kind of reality that could be simply pointed to and recognized at a glance, the discovery would not have required thousands of scientists working ceaselessly over four centuries.

In this exploration I aim for a language that can describe such things as stars and planets and oak trees, but that at another level carries an invitation for a journey to the center of the universe. Arrival at the center is simultaneously a physical and a nonphysical event. Arrival at the center involves understanding what we have learned about the universe, and then incorporating this understanding into our lives.

Learning about the center of the universe is not always a pleasant experience. We will be discussing ideas that sometimes run counter to much of what we ordinarily take as true concerning the world. It's not always pleasant because it can be hard to let go of old assumptions, of preconceived notions, to open our eyes to new horizons. But there is no way around it. Dealing with questions concerning the foundations of the universe requires such an effort.

How convenient it would be if truth were a shiny pebble we could find on the beach and drop in our pockets. Stoop down, pick it up, and it's ours. Certainly some truth can be grasped this way. "I had macaroni for lunch today" requires little effort for comprehension. But deep truths challenge us profoundly. To understand them demands a change in ourselves along with a creative leap of the imagination.

We need to remember that it took some of humanity's most brilliant representatives centuries of uninterrupted investigation to discover the center of the universe. Even after the discovery, some of the most gifted scientists of all, in particular Albert Einstein, failed to grasp what it was they had discovered. If the discovery required so much and shocked some of humanity's finest minds, we should prepare ourselves to put some effort into the work of grasping this new truth.

A new form of consciousness is gradually beginning to emerge among our species. We are astounded by our new awareness, and when we try to speak of it, we discover we have no established way of transmitting it. Perhaps in the future we will have invented a multiplicity of modes for communicating this awareness. But for now, I present the approach I know best, a sustained contemplation on the ways of the universe, on the narrative of evolution we have learned through careful observation and experimentation over the last four hundred years. As we reflect on the dynamics of cosmic evolution and as we begin to align our ways with the ways of the universe, we take the first steps into a new form of human being.

2

A Three-Hundred-Thousand-Year Lineage

Humans have been at the cosmological task a long time. I celebrate the new and startling results of our modern scientific investigation, but we need to remember that we have been involved in the enterprise of cosmology—the exploration of the origin, development, and destiny of the universe—from the very beginning. Most spectacularly we see signs of this in the cave paintings from as far back as twenty thousand years ago in southern Europe, when our ancestors crawled for days on their backs through labyrinthine caves to gather in great underground vaults in order to draw on the walls depictions of the animals that lived in their imagination. Other artifacts of cosmological wonderment reach back perhaps forty thousand years, and some archaeologists surmise that our human ancestors have been gathering in caves as far back as three hundred thousand years ago, haunted even then by the mysteries of the cosmos that filled them with terror and delight.

None of the other animals of the world need to engage in such reflective activities. They enter life and their
basic relationships are a given, written into the genetic
programs that have been fashioned over millions of
years. All except humans know their proper place in the
world. Humans require something different, something
more than genetic codes. Humans require a cultural orientation. We are not born with a fixed and final form to
our orientation in life but must discover and deepen it
through the process of psychic development.

It is not because we have no answers to the question
"What does it mean to be human in this universe?" It is
rather because we have so many different answers that
we need to stop and wonder about the universe in order
to sort out our right and fruitful relationships.

As far back as three hundred millennia ago, humans
huddled together in the night to ponder and to celebrate
the mysteries of the universe in order to find their way
through the great world they inhabited. As history unfolded through the ages, no matter what continent humans lived on, no matter what their culture, the work of
cosmology took place every year and every month and
even every day—around the fires of the African plains, in
the caves of the Eurasian forests, under the brilliant night
sky of the Australian land mass, in the long houses of
North America. In all these places people told the sacred
stories of how the world came to be, and of what it
means to live a noble life within the "Great Holy" that is
the universe.

Modern industrial society does it differently. Questions of ultimate meaning and value are dealt with not in caves or on the open plains, but in churches, mosques, and temples. Here each week billions of humans gather to reflect on their relationship with the divine—whether approached under traditions of God, Allah, Brahma, or the Great Spirit. In all these millions of weekly religious ceremonies, so essential to the health and spirituality of humanity as a whole, one will find a diversity of religious celebrations, but only rarely will one find serious contemplation of these primal human questions *within the context of the actual universe, a universe of stars, topsoil, amphibians, and wetlands.*

Certainly in the world's scriptures and in the religious rituals performed each week there are powerful uses of such words as "water," "sky," "sun," and "rain." But these are employed in a symbolic rather than a literal sense. For instance, "water" might be used as a sign of the saving action of God—but it is not used to point to the Mississippi River. In modern industrial consciousness, the Mississippi River and God live in different domains. God has to do with the gospel of love, with salvation, with care for the poor, with the drama of the Bible, whereas the phrase "the Mississippi River" connotes various "physical" things, like the H_2O molecules, or the dams of the Army Corps of Engineers, or laws dealing with water rights—all of these things understood as separate from matters having to do with God and ultimate questions.

The result is that, within our religions, when we do ponder the deep issues of meaning in the universe, we do so in a context fixed in the time when the classical scriptures were put into written form. We do not worship or contemplate in the context of the universe as we have come to know it over these last centuries, a context that includes the species diversity of the Appalachian Mountains, the million-year development of the enveloping ecosystem, the intricate processes of the human genome, the stellar dynamics that gave birth to Earth five billion years ago, or anything else that is both specific and true concerning the Earth and the universe. All of that—the Earth and universe as they are and as they actually function—is regarded as "science," something separate from the questions of meaning and value that religions deal with.

Modern humans, instead of gathering in caves or cathedrals to dance to poetry and music as a way of learning their place in the universe, sit in classrooms and study science. Certainly such education in the sciences is fundamental for the survival of humanity. The challenges that beset us today will grow ever fiercer for our children and their children, and if we are to deal successfully with those challenges we will need to make use of the best possible science and technology. But nowhere in science education is the meaning of the human in the universe the focus of concern. The ruling assumption is that science is about facts, and it is religion that deals with meaning, purpose, and value.

The tragedy here is that our religions would remain true to their essence if they were to think and work within the larger context of the universe. It would not mean shrinking away from central religious truths. On the contrary, within the context of the dynamics of the developing universe the essential truths of religion could be expressed in a far vaster and more profound form. The recasting would not be a compromise or a diminution but rather a creative fulfillment, the significance of which would go beyond today's most optimistic assessments of the value of religion.

Beginning with the dawn of the modern era, the ancient cosmological enterprise has been broken apart, not as a result of some accidental development but because of ways of thought rooted in the very core values of our modern world. Arguments for a division between science and religion can be found in libraries of philosophical texts from modern thinkers. Defenses of such arguments fill mountains of legal briefs. We are prevented from engaging in the cosmological enterprise precisely because of the institutional processes and thinking of our modern world.

But if humans, in order to become fully human, truly do need to ponder the universe to discover their place in it, and if this three-hundred-thousand-year tradition is rooted in the very nature of our makeup, then in one way or another we will find our way to engage with ideas concerning the proper human role in the universe. And if the institutions of education and religion have, for whatever well-defended reasons, decided to abdicate their role in facilitating this, we need to step forward to fill that role.

How do we learn about the world, the universe? To answer this question we need only reflect on what our children experience over and over again, at night, in a setting similar to that of children in the past who gathered in caves and listened to the chants of the elders. In terms of pure quantities of time, the answer is immediate: the cave has been replaced with the television room and the chant of the elders with the advertisement. One might say that the chant has been replaced with the television *show* but, in essence, the core energy that drives the action and determines whether or not the show will survive the season is the advertisement. That is the reality night after night and season after season. Television's blockbuster sitcoms come and go; the advertisement endures.

What is the effect on our children? Before a child enters first-grade science, and before he or she has entered in any real way into our religious ceremonies, that child will have soaked in thirty thousand advertisements. The time our teenagers spend watching ads is more than their total stay in high school. None of us feel very good about this, but for the most part we just ignore it. It's background. It's just there, part of what's going on. We parents learned to accept it so long ago we hardly think about it.

But imagine how we would feel if we heard about a country that indoctrinated its citizenry with its religious dogmas in such a manner. Actually, it was just such accounts concerning the leaders of the former Soviet Union that outraged citizens of the West for decades— reports that the government was brainwashing young children by subjecting them to Soviet lies, erasing their natural feelings for their parents or for God or for the truth of history and replacing these with the ideological doctrines that would provide support for the dictatorship and enable it to continue its oppressive domination.

Immersed in the religion of consumerism, we refuse to take such comparisons seriously. We tell ourselves soothing clichés, such as that we are free to turn off the television set. We tell ourselves that ads are nothing more than the honest efforts of our corporations to get us interested in their various products. But, as with any reality that we rarely pay any serious attention to, we miss the big picture. The sheer amount of time we spend in the world of the advertisement suggests we might well devote a moment to examining that world more carefully.

Advertisers, of course, are not bad persons with evil designs. They're just doing their job. On the other hand, even they would have to confess that the well-being of our children is not their primary concern. Their objective is to create ads that are successful for their company, and this means getting viewers interested in their product. But already we can see that this is less than desirable. After all, we parents demand that our children's teachers, to take just one example, should have our children's best interests foremost in mind. Such teachers will shape our children when they are young and vulnerable, so of course we want this shaping to be done only by people who care. To hand over so much of our children's young lives to people who obviously do not have our children's well-being foremost in mind is at the very least questionable.

But, on a deeper level, what we need to confront is the power of the advertiser to promulgate a worldview based on dissatisfaction and craving. One of the clichés for how to construct an ad captures the point succinctly: "An ad's job is to make them unhappy with what they have."

We rarely think of ads as being shaped by explicit worldviews, and that is precisely why they are so effective. The last thing we want to think about as we're lying on the couch relaxing is the philosophy behind the ad. So, as we soak it all up, it sinks down deeply into our psyche. And if this takes place in the adult soul, imagine what happens to the psyches of our children, who have none of our protective cynicisms but who take in the ad's imagery and message as if they were coming from a trusted parent or teacher.

Advertisers in the corporate world are of course offered lucrative recompense, and, with that financial draw, our corporations attract humans with the highest IQs. And our best artistic talent. And any sports hero or movie star they want to buy. Combining so much brain power and social status with sophisticated electronic graphics and the most penetrating psychological techniques, these teams of highly skilled adults descend upon all of us, even upon children not yet in school, with the simple desire to create in us a dissatisfaction with our lives. It's hard to imagine any child having the capacity to survive such a lopsided contest, especially when it's carried out ten thousand times a year, with no cultural deterrent capable of blocking out the consumerism virus. Could even one child in the whole world endure that onslaught and

come out unscathed? Extremely doubtful. Put it all together and you can see why it's no great mystery that
consumerism has become the dominant world faith of
every continent of the planet today.

The point I wish to make is not just that our children
are such easy prey. It's not just that the rushing river of
advertisements determines the sorts of shoes our children desire, the sorts of clothes and toys and games and
sugar cereals that they must have. It's not just the unhappiness they are left with whenever they cannot have
such commodities, an unhappiness that in many cases
leads to aggressive violence of the worst kind in order to
obtain by force what their parents will not or cannot give
them. All of this is of great concern, but the point I wish
to focus on here has to do with the question of how we
learn about the world.

Advertisements are where our children are first ex-
posed to cosmology, to a basic view of the world's meaning, which amounts to their primary religious faith,
though unrecognized as such. I use the word "faith"
here to mean cosmology on the personal level. Faith
refers to that which a person holds to be the ultimate
truth of things. The advertisement is our culture's primary vehicle for providing our children with a worldview
that will shape their personal cosmologies. As this awful
fact sinks into awareness, the first healthy response is one
of denial. It is just too horrible to think that we live in a
culture that has replaced authentic spiritual development with the advertisement's crass materialism. And yet
when one compares the pitiful efforts our educational

systems devote to moral development with the colossal energies we pour into advertising, it is like comparing a high school football game with World War II.

Perhaps the more recalcitrant children will require upward of a hundred thousand ads before they cave in and accept consumerism's basic worldview. But eventually we all get the message. It's a simple cosmology, told with great effect and delivered a billion times each day: *humans exist to work at jobs, to earn money in order to buy things.* The image of the ideal human is also deeply set and reinforced in our minds by the unending onslaughts of the ad. The ideal is not Jesus or Socrates. Forget all about Rachel Carson or Confucius or Martin Luther King, Jr., and all their suffering and love and wisdom. In the propaganda of the ad, the ideal people, the fully human people, are relaxed and carefree—drinking Pepsis around a pool, unencumbered by thoughts concerning the nature of goodness, undisturbed by the suffering that could be alleviated if humans were committed to justice. We never see any of that.

None of what I have said here concerning ads and their effects on children will be news to those educators who for decades have been lamenting this oppressive situation. But I bring up the issue for two reasons.

The fact that consumerism has become the dominant world faith is largely invisible to us, so it is helpful to understand clearly that to hand our children over to the consumer culture is to place them in the care of the planet's most sophisticated religious preachers. If those bizarre cults we read about in the papers used even one-tenth of one percent of the dazzling manipulation of our advertisers, they would be hounded by the federal law enforcement agencies and thrown into jail straightaway. But in most of the world we are so blinded by the all-encompassing and ceaseless propaganda that we never think to confront the advertisers and demand that they cease. On the contrary, as if cult members ourselves, we pay them high salaries and hand over our children in the bargain.

The second reason for bringing up the advertisement's hold on us has to do with my fundamental aim in presenting the new cosmology. If we come to an awareness of the way in which the materialism of the advertisement is our culture's primary way for shaping our children, and if we find this unacceptable, we are left with the task of inventing new ways of introducing our children, our teenagers, our young adults, our middle-aged adults, and our older adults to the universe. The ideas presented here on the new cosmology are grounded in our contemporary scientific understanding of the universe and nourished by our more ancient spiritual convictions concerning its meaning. These notes, then, are a first step out of the religion of consumerism and into a way of life based upon the conviction that we live in a sacred universe.

3

The Whirling Solar System

The earliest cosmologies regarded Earth as the center of the cosmos. So common was this idea among the peoples of the various continents that the notion of Earth's centrality in the universe might be considered a primal cosmological intuition of humanity. In one particular expression of this, the Western European, we can still enjoy a supreme expression of the geocentric cosmology splashed across the ceiling of the Sistine Chapel. There Michelangelo tells the story of creation in nine panels. The story begins with God fashioning the Earth and ends with the human drama of sin and salvation taking place at the center of the universe. Other classical civilizations had similar geocentric conceptions, all of which differ radically from our current understanding of the universe.

The modern scientific endeavor began with the destruction of humanity's customary geocentric cosmology. In 1543, Nicolaus Copernicus, an obscure Polish astronomer, announced that the Sun was the center of the cosmos. "Announced" is actually not the best word. People were surely announcing all sorts of things back then, just like today. Some people were announcing that the Earth was flat. Others announced that the Sun was the god Ra. The difference in Copernicus's case was that he provided a book with his announcement, and the book provided a way to understand that the Sun was the center around which the planets moved.

What we need to appreciate here is the audacity of the whole operation. For maybe hundreds of thousands of years, humans had assumed as an obvious fact that the Earth was the center of the universe. Those earlier humans would have been deeply confused by any suggestion that the Sun resided at the center and that the Earth was spinning around it. Such an idea is, to say the least, far from obvious.

For the naive or uncritical mind, the Sun is this hot thing up in the sky that travels around the Earth every day. We can't tell how big it is, but it couldn't be that big, because you can block it out entirely with just your thumb. The Earth, in contrast, is the whole world! It's a place of great oceans and vast mountain ranges and terrifying blizzards! In the minds of early humans, the Earth was obviously the most stable place in this universe. It stood still year after year while all the seasons came and went and the stars and planets and Sun and moon whirled about it. To move from this naive and entirely natural understanding to a view that is profoundly "unnatural" and counterintuitive certainly seemed like a strange and dangerous step to take.

The greatness of Copernicus is that with his book he provided a process by which the most advanced thinkers of Europe could come to grasp this new, subtle, disturbing, and amazing truth: the Sun resides in the center of the solar system while the Earth and Mars and Jupiter and all the planets circle about it. To gauge the greatness of Copernicus and the other pioneers of modern scientific understanding, one needs to appreciate their achievements from the perspective of biological evolution. From the time they began fashioning their first tools, human beings required two million years to come up with a way of seeing through the naive and natural assumptions about the Earth and Sun in order to arrive at an understanding more firmly rooted in the actual operation of the universe. Early modern scientists then didn't just offer yet another cultural idea; they broke with a two-million-year tradition in human knowing, for they introduced knowledge that was so far from common sense it even flatly opposed what seemed unquestionably true.

The monumental nature of Copernicus's breakthrough can be appreciated directly. Though all of us now accept the fact that the Earth moves around the Sun, this truth has actually been appropriated *in a bodily way* by only a tiny segment of humanity. The cultural storms surrounding reports of the Sun's centrality have come and gone, and yet most of us watching a sunset have an experience similar to what medieval people experienced when they watched a sunset, which was the same as what people in the classical civilizations experienced, as well as those back still further, in the Neolithic and Paleolithic eras. In fact, this common experience of sunset is just what any primate would have experienced any time since the very beginning of primate life, seventy million years ago. We have all watched the Sun descend and then drop below the dark, unmoving horizon. If asked afterward what we were doing, we say, "I was watching the Sun go down." But if asked to explain what had happened, we would say, "Well, you know, the Earth is spinning so it just appears as if the Sun is going down."

In order to move from ordinary consciousness to a new kind of awareness, we need a transformation of our experience that takes place concurrently with our acquisition of knowledge. It is not enough simply to learn more facts and acquire knowledge about the universe. Something much deeper and more difficult is necessary. The challenge is difficult precisely because of the counterintuitive nature of scientific discoveries. Science arrives at truths that are not part of our innate understanding and experience, and thus scientific truths often appear strange and unnatural. But so long as such truths are left to dangle outside us as abstractions, we are condemned to live a split life.

The problem can be concisely stated. Our primal perceptual habits of consciousness cause us to see the Sun "going down." Our observational and theoretical studies, on the other hand, tell us that the Earth revolves around the Sun. What is needed is a transformative process whereby we can learn to see and to feel the world in a way that is congruent with what is actually happening. Such a transformation would enable us to transcend the split modern condition of experiencing the world one way while knowing that the truth of the world is otherwise.

In the science departments of our universities, *change of perception* is rarely included as a primary aim of the curriculum. The central focus is the production and accumulation of knowledge. Learning to experience a dynamic, evolving universe does occur, but always in a haphazard manner and as a byproduct. What I am suggesting is that in the twenty-first century a transformation of subjectivity might become an explicit goal of education, not as a replacement for the traditional goal of conceptual knowledge but as its culmination.

My aim here is not to hand over information as if I were passing on a sheaf of papers from me to you. My aim is to present information on the birthplace of the universe in a way that invites you to participate in an inner transformation. It would be a great thing if a person learned the facts of the new story. Even greater would be to take the first steps into *living* the new story.

A significant event in our evolution provides an image for the challenge we are confronting here. If we go back far enough in time we find that all mammals had eyes on the sides of their heads. When they looked at something, they saw with one eye at a time, in much the same way as a horse or a rhino does today. But eventually a particular group of mammals found themselves living in the trees of a forest and things began to change.

Faced with the challenge of functioning in a radically different world, surrounded by thick tangles of branches and vines, these mammals began to change. Over a very long period of time, their eyes gradually migrated to the fronts of their faces; this led to the development of stereoscopic vision with its depth perception. The new mammals were the primates, and their ability to judge with great accuracy the distance from hand to branch was critical to their survival as, through the ages, they spread through the forests of the continents. If we consider the primate line as a whole, we can think of their journey as a single process whereby they learned to successfully adjust to the new world that surrounded them.

We are similarly challenged today. We are over seven billion humans, and we need to learn to live with one another and with all Earth's life communities in a mutually enhancing way. We fail at the present time precisely because we fail to see and understand what it is that surrounds us. In order to be able to see, we need nothing like the anatomical changes that enabled the primates to survive but, rather, a new mind and a new story that will enable us to inhabit successfully the quantum evolutionary cosmos. We need to learn to experience directly the more subtle complexities of the seamless whole that is nature, or cosmos, and that includes the events of our moments as well as the great events of the past and the yet-to-be events that will follow our moment now. When we learn to experience our world in such a manner, we will have crossed into a new way of being human, just as the primates crossed into a new way of being mammals.

To take a beginning step, I'd like to suggest focusing on the experience of a sunset. Any person who wants to can transform her perceptual habits and can learn to see, in a direct experiential way, the Earth rotating away from the Sun. The simplest way to do this is to go outside half an hour before "sunset," at a time when Venus is low on the horizon. It would be helpful if another planet, such as Jupiter or Mars, were also visible, but that is not necessary. Finally, bring along a child. She will probably get there first, and her glow of discovery will assist you in arriving at your own.

Begin by focusing your attention on Venus and, as you do so, keep the model of the solar system in mind as a way of organizing your experience. So, either by speaking out loud or in the silence of your thoughts, review the basic facts: "Venus is 65 million miles from the Sun, about a third closer to the Sun than the Earth, which is 93 million miles from the Sun. And there, higher up in my field of vision, is Jupiter, 480 million miles from the Sun. All three of us are moving in a single plane around the Sun." And so forth. The actual numbers are not even necessary here. What needs to be kept in mind is the simple fact that the distances are enormous and that—in terms of the three planets—Venus is closest to the Sun, then Earth, then Jupiter, and all three move in the same plane about the Sun.

Simply by focusing on the experience and viewing it through the theoretical model of the solar system's form, there will come a wonderful moment when you enter into it all at once: you feel in an experiential, imaginative, and direct way the Earth slowly turning away from the Sun. You have a sense of the plane in which the planets move, and even a beginning recognition of the great distance to Venus. You will also feel, perhaps for the first time in your life, the immensity of the Earth as it rolls away from the great Sun. A single surprising shudder might pass through you as you realize you are standing on the back of something like a cosmic whale, one that is slowly rotating its great bulk on the surface of an unseen ocean.

It is true that, soon afterward, you might snap right back into your everyday way of experiencing the world. But if even for a moment you enter this larger experience of the world, you will be able to enter it again more easily in the future. The primary gateways are dawn and dusk, but as you grow in competence you can learn to experience yourself on the whirling Earth amid the enveloping solar system at any time and in any place. In each such moment you remain of course an individual person on the planet, but you become as well part of a living planet encircling a star.

As you learn to feel directly the immensity of the Earth rotating away from the Sun, you can then take the further step of feeling the Earth swinging around the Sun.

Although we say, "The Earth revolves around the Sun," the truth is slightly different. The Sun is also moving, though not as much as the Earth is moving. An image that can help in understanding this is that of the hammer throw in Olympic competition. Here a person swings a hammer around and around and then flings it through the air. A careful examination of the movement would show that the human is not at the fixed center of the spinning motion but that the human and the disk both revolve about their common center of gravity. The human doesn't move in as big a circle as the hammer because the human weighs much more than the hammer; and, in a similar way, the Sun does not move anywhere near as much as the Earth, because the Sun is so much heavier than the Earth. Nevertheless, the Sun does move in a small circle as both the Sun and Earth revolve about their common center of gravity. The point of their center of gravity is inside the Sun, but it is not at the Sun's center. This is because the point of their center of gravity is the center of mass of all the objects in the solar system combined, and the position of this point shifts slightly depending on the position of the planets in their orbits.

If, again at dawn or dusk, you place yourself in the same setting, with Venus in the sky and a child at your side, you can get your first real taste of the Earth's movement around the Sun and the Sun's tiny wobble in response.

One additional fact will aid you here. The size of the Sun is approximately a million times the size of the Earth. Thus, if you start by considering Earth's immensity, and you now imagine that hot bright object on the horizon as containing a million Earths, you can begin to feel the way in which the massiveness of the Sun whips the Earth and all the other planets through their annual arcs. The crucial step here is to be aware of the fact of the Sun's gravitational power. Earth is one immense planet, and it is being whipped around the Sun *by the power of the Sun*. This is something the Sun is *doing* in every instant of every day. We are held by the Sun. If the Sun released us from our bond with it, we would sail off into deep space.

As before, a new awareness will come in a sudden shift, where a door opens and you feel yourself sliding into an unexpected and disorienting place. It is disorienting, not in the sense of an irritated confusion—for the experience is not at all irritating but on the contrary is actually breathtaking; it is disorienting in the sense of a bottom dropping away, as if for the first time in your life you have closed your eyes and leaped into a body of cool water and are suddenly turning about weightless without toes or fingers touching any ground.

Words are pathetically inadequate to convey this experience. Modern English as a living language was created over the last five centuries by humans who had not had this particular experience of the cosmos, so how likely is it that English would contain the verbs, adjectives, metaphors, and rhetorical images necessary to convey it? There is no linguistic formulation that would substitute for your direct experience here. To fully understand, you have to sit down and leave yourself open to engage with the universe.

But if you do so, you will become one of a very small number of humans *who actually live in the solar system*. Most humans live not on the Earth that rotates and revolves about the Sun. We live rather in a fantasy that regards the Earth as a fixed place, where the ground is always stationary; that regards the planet as somehow resting on a great slab of cement. But to contemplate the solar system until you feel the great Earth turning away from the Sun and until you feel this immense planet being swung around its massive cosmic partner is to dip your feet into an ocean of wonder as you take a first step in experiencing the actual universe and solar system and Earth.

Of course, all of this is an ephemoral realization without cultural support. Our new cosmological orientation, even if deeply felt, will soon be buffeted by the simplistic materialism dominant in our industrial societies and transformed back into the familiar Earth-centered fantasy that prevails in our world. That's where we find ourselves today. Our tasting of the wonder of the universe will be sporadic and brief. But, even if such encounters are ephemeral, they will nevertheless enable us to experience ourselves, perhaps for the first time, as soaring around a star that floats in the vast ocean of the cosmos.

4

Cosmology and Ecstasy

Since my educational training and professional work are in science, I inevitably share all the shortcomings of my tribe, and thus I tend to overemphasize the intellectual side of the experience of connecting with the evolving universe. But if the task of initiating humans into the experience of the universe were solely intellectual, we could accomplish it with our science classes. Cosmology, though consonant with science, is not science. It is a wisdom tradition with the aim of transforming the human being from an industrial consciousness to a cosmological consciousness. Initiation into a new form of humanity always involves emotions and intuitions as well as intellectual concepts.

When I first began discussing some of the ecstatic feelings and new vistas that inevitably accompany an experience of our evolving and expanding universe, I was often asked if I used psychedelics. My questioners were intrigued by the similarities between what they had experienced and what I was teaching about the universe. I told them I had had no such experiences. I went on to say I was not happy with the idea that people might dismiss what I was teaching as nothing more than a wild tale from someone using a psychoactive substance. Science has discovered a whole range of stunning truths about the universe. I wanted everyone to be clear that these scientific discoveries were the focus in my teaching.

But, as the years went by and as the questions about the similarities continued, I came to a new understanding. The crucial insight belongs to Thomas Berry, who explained to me that in industrial society there is an inverse relationship between outer knowledge and inner experience. Based on his extensive scholarship, he made the claim that the scientific industrial society had more knowledge of the universe than any previous culture, and yet we lived in the tiniest psychic space of any group in human history. He asserted that this shrunken psychic state is the mirror image of industrial society's assumption that the universe is a collection of inert objects.

Once we convinced ourselves that we live in a dead universe, and once we concluded that other animals are nothing more than things, we condemned ourselves. We came to believe that all previous humans were simply ignorant children. We moderns were the adult humans because we know so much. We assume that the universe is meaningless. It is for this reason that depression is a regular feature in every consumer society. We are swamped by a vast loneliness that has soaked into every stratum of our society.

Isolation and alienation are false states of mind in an evolving universe. We exist within intimate relationships that reach back to the primordial energies now suffusing each cell of our bodies. The pathways for experiencing ecstatic participation in cosmic creativity are multiple. All of them involve a journey that begins in the isolation of industrial consciousness and moves forward to the ecstasy of an enveloping community of beings. For some, the pathway is contemplation. For others it is service to those who are suffering. For others the pathway is psychoactive plants and mushrooms. Others find it in artistic and musical expression. For still others, it is a journey that begins with a study of history or science.

If we take the three hundred thousand years of human development as a guide, the creative task of our time is to invent cultural forms for initiating human beings into an experience of participation with oceans, animals, stars. Experiencing the new cosmology will lead to a zest for life, a psychic energy for beginning each day with joy. The modern system of education, with its exclusive focus on conceptual knowledge, will be replaced by qualitatively new practices that awaken human beings to their larger destinies as participants in the creative cosmos. Bold and daring initiatives are necessary. There are no experts for this task. It calls not for expertise but for creativity.

5

The Sun as the Center

Some scholars, even some who are otherwise respectable scientists, make the mistake of claiming that twentieth-century science has proven Copernicus wrong. Not that the medieval geocentric model of the universe was correct; rather, both that model and Copernicus's heliocentric model are false. The argument goes as follows: Copernicus thought that the Sun was the center of the cosmos, but we now know that the Sun is only one of trillions of stars in the universe, none of which is qualitatively different from all the rest. So Copernicus's notion couldn't have been correct.

In a superficial sense, this argument is flawless, for certainly it is true that Copernicus had no idea of how vast the universe is. His data restricted his thinking to a much, much smaller cosmos, and he would have been astounded to learn the dimensions of the universe we now deal with. But the more important point, one that is missed entirely by this line of reasoning, is that Copernicus discovered *that the Sun is the center of the dynamics of our solar system.* Nothing learned about the universe since the time of his death changes this truth in the least. Though with Isaac Newton and Albert Einstein and Richard Feynman and Barbara McClintock we have enlarged and deepened our scientific understanding in tremendous ways, Copernicus's radical insight concerning the centrality of the Sun continues undisturbed inside all our contemporary theories about the universe.

Actually, in the five centuries since Copernicus's death, our ongoing exploration of the universe has led us to an even deeper understanding of how the Sun is at the center of the solar system. We have already touched upon this in our consideration of the size of the Sun. The Earth is just the tiniest fraction of the Sun's size—only a millionth of the Sun's volume. The Earth and the other planets are just wisps silently sailing through a space suffused with our star's brightness. A human with a cosmological education should learn that truth and should feel it directly in a bodily and imaginative way.

The discovery I would like to examine here has to do with energy. Using the detailed understanding of atomic and nuclear physics discovered and developed in the twentieth century, we have learned something never even suspected by the greatest thinkers in all of human history, including Copernicus himself, and Galileo, Aristotle, Confucius, Plato, and all the others. The Sun, each second, transforms four million tons of itself into light. Each second, a huge chunk of the Sun vanishes into radiant energy that soars away in all directions. In our own experience we have perhaps watched candles burn down or have seen wood consumed by flames leaving behind only ashes, but nothing in all our human experience compares to this astounding blaze that engulfs oceans of matter each day.

The ancient Greeks conveyed their deepest truths through poetry and myth, and thus bequeathed to us the stories of Apollo, Hephaestus, Aphrodite, Athena, and Zeus. Were we at that same stage of human consciousness, such myths would enable us, as they enabled the Greeks, to enter into a rich relationship with the powers in the universe. But they no longer work in the same way for us. Although such stories are false in any literal sense concerning their descriptions of the universe, psychologists such as C. G. Jung and others have rescued them from the scrap heap of history by explaining to us their psychological relevance. We are thus condemned by our scientific knowledge to regard them, ultimately, as "myths," as fictions, as clever ways to teach psychological truths.

Thus, when we come to the fact of the Sun's massive transformation into energy, we are stymied. We have no myths or epic poems that celebrate this extraordinary truth. It all collapses down to just another fact from the new science. And it is so alien, this profligate and monstrous discharge of energy. If anything, we distance ourselves from it. It is yet another forbidding truth about the inhuman universe, and we unconsciously commit to sealing ourselves away from the universe.

Here is yet another gateway through which the cosmological imagination can walk toward a new synthesis of science and religion. In the case of the Sun, we have a new understanding of the cosmological meaning of sacrifice. The Sun is, with each second, giving itself over to become energy that we, with every meal, partake of. We so rarely reflect on this basic truth from biology, and yet its spiritual significance is supreme. The Sun converts itself into a flow of energy that photosynthesis changes into plants that are consumed by animals. So for four million years, humans have been feasting on the Sun's energy stored in the form of wheat or maize or reindeer as each day the Sun dies as Sun and is reborn as Earth's vitality. Those photons are in fact what powers the vast human enterprise, and every child of ours needs to learn the simple truth that the energy flowing through her is the energy of the Sun. We adults should organize things so that her face can shine with the radiance of the Sun.

During the modern period when crass materialism came to dominate, such a suggestion as this last one would be considered "mere poetry." We simply did not know that the actual energy coursing through our respiratory and nervous systems was bestowed upon us by the Sun and that our own vitality is a natural evolutionary development of the Sun's vitality. So, instead of introducing our young people to the Sun, we cut them off from the Sun. That is, instead of awakening in our children an understanding of this primordial relationship that would shine forth from their faces with the radiance of the Sun, we unknowingly and tragically snuffed it out. They were left with our conviction that the universe is a collection of dead objects, and so it has gone from generation to generation up until today.

In the cosmology of the twenty-first century, the Sun's lavish bestowal of energy can be regarded as the spectacular manifestation of an underlying impulse pervading the universe. In the star, this impulse reveals itself in the ongoing giving away of energy. In the human heart, it is felt as the urge to devote one's life to the well-being of the larger community.

In a culture in which cosmology is alive, children are taught by the Sun and Moon, by the rainfall and the starlight, by the salmon run and the germinating seed. It has been so long since we moderns have lived in such a world that it is difficult to picture, but we can just now begin to imagine what it might be like for our children, or for our children's children.

They will wake up a few moments before dawn and go out into the gray light. As they're yawning away the last of their sleep and as the Earth slowly rotates back into the great cone of light from the Sun, they will hear the story of the Sun's gift. How five billion years ago the hydrogen atoms, created at the birth of the universe, came together to form our great Sun that now pours out this same primordial energy and has done so from the beginning of its existence. How some of this energy is gathered up by life to swim in the oceans and to sing in the forests. And how some of it has been incorporated into the human venture, so that human beings themselves are able to stand here, are able to yawn, are able to think only because coursing through their blood lines are molecules energized by the Sun.

And then they will hear the simple truth about the necessity of such a bestowal. If we shine brightly today it is only because this same energy was shining brightly in the Sun a month ago. Even as we breath out, our energy dissipates and we need to be replenished all over again by the Sun's gift. If the Sun were suddenly to stop transforming itself into energy, all the plants would die as the Earth's temperature plummeted hundreds of degrees below zero. In our veins and our flesh, all the heat-giving molecules would grow cold as we and everything else became hard as frozen dust.

The Sun's story will find its climax in a story from the human family of those men and women whose lives have manifested the same generosity and whose sacrifice has enabled others to reach fulfillment. If through the ages the various cultures have admired people who poured out their creative energies so that others might live, they were admiring such humans for being true to the nature of the energy that filled them.

Human generosity is possible only because at the center of the solar system a magnificent stellar generosity pours forth free energy day and night without stop, without complaint, and without the slightest hesitation. This is the way of the universe. This is the way of life. And this is the way in which each of us joins this cosmological lineage when we accept the Sun's gift of energy and transform it into creative action that will enable the community to flourish.

Of course, over the years, as the Sun's story is repeated in its various forms, there will be a good deal of repetition, and listeners will sometimes be bored and distracted. This is to be expected, because the story has to do not with entertainment but with education. Moral education in particular rests upon holding in mind, over long periods of time, the magnificent achievements of fourteen billion years of creativity.

By reminding ourselves of the possibilities of true greatness and true nobility of spirit, we excite the energies necessary for our fulfillment. The challenge of moral and spiritual achievement is not something that can be dealt with in an hour on the weekend. The task of transformation must be the way we start each day as we remind ourselves of the revelation that is the Sun.

Through repetition and through years of deepening, our children and our children's children will be provided with a way to escape the lures of deceit, and greed, hatred, and self-doubt, for they will begin each morning and live each day inside the simple truth: a gorgeous living Earth circling light as a feather around the great roaring generosity of the Sun.

6

Looking Down on the Milky Way

Even if the discovery of the birthplace of the universe is the greatest of the twentieth century or of all time, it is meaningless until it comes alive within us. The discovery itself was the result not of some accidental action but of deliberate and sustained effort over time. So too with the meaning of that discovery. It is easy for someone to become momentarily fascinated or titillated by the wild data of the new story of the universe, but it is another thing altogether to absorb its meaning into the center of one's being. What is needed is embodiment. What is needed is a transformation of humanity from the form it takes today into forms congruent with the ways of the universe. Such a transformation will take place in those individuals who have the courage, imagination, and energy necessary for the journey.

To study the new cosmology is to have your consciousness transformed. One of the more depressing insights in this transformation is to realize how efficient we have been in sealing ourselves and our children off from any contact with the universe. Consider, for instance, the trillion galaxies. We have learned so many awesome things about the galaxies of the universe, and yet how many of us have any direct experience of galaxies? Certainly some of us study galaxies in science class, but without a primal encounter with a galaxy, what good is such abstract knowledge?

In order to really learn about galaxies and about the birthplace of the universe, we need to struggle with the way our children are largely encapsulated in human artifice. I am not now suggesting a return to primitive lifestyles, or a rejection of technology, or a romantic back-to-nature fantasy about abandoning cities and living in communes. What we need is just the simple recognition that when we deprive ourselves and our children of direct contact with the numinous powers that fill the universe, we choose a diminished existence.

All industrial societies are captured, to varying degrees, by the idea frozen in the Rogers Centre in Toronto (originally called the SkyDome), a huge sports stadium with an attached hotel. Humans can be completely encased in this ingenious mechanical structure for weeks at a time. Once inside they don't see the great sky or the blazing sun; they don't smell the sweet Earth or touch the rough bark of the trees; they don't hear the wind blow across the fields or the splash of a fish at twilight in a darkening lake. All those things are traded for a life in contact with cement, glass, AstroTurf, video displays, steel, and plastic. Take away the glitz and the crowds and what you have is the daily experience so many millions of our children wake up to each morning. When we think about this, we may begin to suspect that trading Sun and Moon and animals and galaxies for an ever-present iPhone may not be such a great deal after all.

If you've never had an experience of a galaxy, you have before you one of the great opportunities of life on Earth. All that is needed is to journey forty or fifty miles to get out from under urban pollution. If you live in the country, even better, for you are already there. Go with some friends, take a couple of blankets, a thermos or two, and as soon as night falls lie on your back and behold that path of milky light that runs from the horizon on one side clear through the great vault of the heavens all the way down to the horizon on the other side. This is the Milky Way Galaxy, our home.

In an ultimate sense, we know so little about the universe, so little about the dark past, so little about the future that is to come. But we do know that as we wonder at this great milky path surrounding us in the night, we are entering into an experience that billions of humans back through time have shared. From every place on the planet, and in every period of history, humans have experienced awe while contemplating this great light that encircles the world.

The beginning and the end of human existence is awe. We have that in common with all those countless ancestors who have been mesmerized by the night's beauty. They had their ways of explaining to themselves what it all meant. And now we too have a way, a new way, of explaining what we see. In every case, awe is inherent. And if the explanation is a good one, the awe will only deepen. The primary purpose of our explanations is not to eliminate awe but to bring us into a more intimate understanding of the mysteries enveloping us and thus carry us still deeper into the ocean of beauty in which we find ourselves.

In the modern period we have become so puffed up with our sense of superiority concerning science's explanations of the universe we have not even noticed that we have stopped wondering about the stars. It has seemed reasonable to stop paying attention to the cosmos. Why wonder about something when we are convinced it is only a machine? Why pay attention to something when we have the mathematics to explain it? We have regarded a scientific explanation as something that removes the mystery, so that over time we have tricked ourselves into thinking that the mathematical explanations of phenomena are more significant than the phenomena! Believe that, and before long you're living in the SkyDome.

The beginning and the end are primordial encounters with the great abyss of beauty that we call the universe. Not to enter moments of awe, not to wonder over the majesty of the universe, not to live each day—at least for a moment or two!—floating inside the colossal and intimate mystery, is to live a life that is deprived, a life that is vulnerable to fundamental distortions.

As we lie on our backs, mesmerized by the great Milky Way above us, we can ponder our recent discoveries in order to deepen this encounter. None of the billions of humans preceding us could experience the Milky Way as we can today, for, when we contemplate the trail of milky light stretching across the sky, we know this light comes from the three hundred billion stars of the Milky Way Galaxy. We see these stars as a soft band of light because of the shape of our galaxy.

In its three-dimensional form, the Milky Way is sometimes compared to a pancake that has a bulge at the center (the bulge is mostly made up of dust and old stars). Another image sometimes used is that of an egg in a frying pan, the yoke as the bulge and the egg white as the larger and thinner sections emanating out from the hub. But I like to think of the Milky Way Galaxy as a gigantic manta ray. A manta ray is a fish with a flattened body, a slight bulge at the center, and two great dark wings for propelling itself through the oceans. The principal advantage in using the manta ray as a metaphor for seeing the Milky Way Galaxy is the ease with which the manta ray reminds us that the Milky Way is not sitting on anything. The Milky Way is soaring effortlessly through the dark universe just as the manta ray glides weightlessly through the seas.

Earth is halfway out from the thick center, and it is inside the Orion arm. Since we are swirling around inside this galactic manta ray, at night we see stars in whatever direction we look, but when our line of sight is straight across the plane of the Milky Way's body we see many more stars, so many that their light commingles into that shimmering path. This milky path continues all around the Earth. We cannot see it during the day because of the overpowering presence of the Sun. But as we lie on our backs, imagining Earth within the body of the galaxy and the milky path stretching from one horizon clear across the sky to the opposite horizon and beyond, we can begin to experience the Earth as floating within this great body, the Milky Way, which itself is floating in the great body of the universe.

We now need to experiment with altering the basic patterns that have been entrenched in the consciousness of primates for at least seventy million years. As we lie on our backs viewing the Milky Way, we might become aware of the fact that an implicit assumption framing our experience is that of "looking up at the stars." This unconscious attitude is biologically rooted, for the sense of an up-down direction is coded into the psyche of primates. A chimpanzee awakening in the night in its nest in the trees needs to be instantly oriented by the up-down axis. Put another way, all the ancestral chimpanzees who needed more than a couple of seconds to figure out which way was up have long since met their demise by falling down.

Further strengthening our sense of up-down is the cultural coding worked out over millennia in terms of which the stars and heaven and God are "up" and the Earth is "below." As discussed earlier, countless generations of humans regarded Earth as the fixed place at the center of the universe above which the heavens turned. Such a worldview simply articulates the implicit biological orientation of all primates. If an orangutan could speak, it too would regard the stars as far above, up in the sky; and if it were lying on its back on a field of grass at night, it too would think it was looking up at the stars.

So what do we do now, when our knowledge transcends the genetically and culturally coded assumptions concerning "up"? How do we orient ourselves in the universe now that we know a round Earth is sailing around the Sun, and that the Sun is a star similar to the other three hundred billion stars of the Milky Way, and that the idea of "up," which we might experience on Earth, has nothing to do with the dynamics of the galaxy as it spins its stars in their great orbits?

As you lie on your back beholding the Milky Way, see if you can imaginatively free yourself from seventy million years of conditioning regarding our place in the universe. Such imaginative work is one of the great joys of being human, and it is at the core of all great achievements in art, science, and civilization as a whole. Imagine the Earth floating in space, and instead of picturing your own place on the "top" part of the Earth, arrange the picture in your mind so that you are positioned on the "bottom" of the Earth.

Now, as you lie there, imagine yourself peering down into the great chasm of the night sky. If your imagination is strong enough, you can enter quickly into a new experience. Otherwise it might take some time, but the moment will come, in a rapid reorganization of phenomena, when all those stars will be experienced as down below—far, far below—and the amazing feeling accompanying this experience will be a sense of surprise that you are not falling down there to join them. But of course you don't fall. You hover in space, gazing down into the vault of stars, suspended there because of your bond with Earth.

Earth's gravitational power holds you, and you feel the strength of this bond in the pressure felt in your shoulders and along your back and buttocks and legs. We normally think of this pressure as coming from our "weight" but, in a strictly scientific sense, no being has any intrinsic weight. Rather, all bodies are capable of entering into gravitational interactions; and for us, the dominant gravitational interaction we experience is with Earth. It is not some intrinsic weight that keeps us here. If the gravitational power of Earth and Sun were suddenly to vanish, we would, with ever increasing velocity, soar away in a great rush down into that dark chasm of stars below us. It's the Earth's hold that keeps us suspended above the stars.

So, as you lie there feeling yourself hovering within this gravitational bond while peering down at the billions of stars drifting in the infinite chasm of space, you will have allowed yourself to enter an experience of the universe that is not just human and not just biological. You will have entered a relationship from a galactic perspective, becoming for a moment a part of the Milky Way Galaxy, experiencing what it's like to be the Milky Way Galaxy.

The path of white that you are dreamily contemplating has the power of the gods. The destiny of Earth and the Sun and the planets and your own body is controlled by that Milky Way sweeping through the night sky. That milky white path is whipping the entire solar system around the outer edge of the galaxy at a speed of 180 miles per second. As you lie there and count to twenty, all the animals and forests and the entire Earth and Jupiter and the asteroids and even the great Sun are flung a distance equal to the width of the North American continent.

I sometimes wonder over the fact that if I could lift a ton of bricks and toss them a few feet I would be on every TV screen in the world. But Earth is a billion trillion times more massive than a ton of bricks, and the Sun is a million times huger than Earth. And all of that and more is not just lifted up and tossed a few feet but has been flung 180 miles each second of the day, all day long, all year long, for five billion years now. The origin of such titanic power is that milky white path that we contemplate as we are held suspended over its immense powers. Why would people watch me lift a ton of bricks when they could behold each night a dynamism that is a quintillion times mightier?

We modern people have said some very questionable things about what a great advance scientific humans represent. To fall into the trite conceptions about how limited earlier peoples were is an easy mistake for a consumer to make—I mean, after all, they had no dishwashers, no TVs, no Mac computers. But they did understand something central that escapes us modern and postmodern people. We have forgotten what it was and, even worse, we've forgotten that we've forgotten. In their work of orienting themselves within the great determining powers of the universe, primal people achieved an integration with a living Earth that we can only guess at.

They had little technology, they had no electrical appliances, they were vulnerable in a thousand ways, but they lived in forms of consciousness, or cosmovisions, far beyond what we normally experience in our daily lives within our industrial cages. With each morning they awoke to a numinous universe. With each morning they awoke to a reality we usually experience only in our dreams where we are swept up into a great adventure involving the entire universe. If we do not know fully what it was that our ancestors experienced, we can appreciate what indigenous peoples today have brought forward in their resilience. We can hope that as we develop our own cosmological relationships with the powers of the universe, we too will wake up one morning in an enchanted world in which we have a role to play and are able to speak to our children about all these ultimate things.

7

A Large-Scale View of Space and Time

In a superficial sense, everyone lives in the universe because we're all physically here. But in an intellectual or spiritual or emotional sense, most of us live elsewhere. This is indeed a strange situation. It is a deformation that humans have succumbed to over and over again throughout history.

Sophocles made a study of the interesting possibility of a split life in his drama *Oedipus Rex*. This is the story of a man who arrives in a kingdom one day and, through an unfortunate string of events, ends up killing the king and marrying the queen, completely ignorant of the terrible truth that the king is his father and the queen his mother.

We could say that even though Oedipus was made king of Thebes, he did not actually live in the kingdom of Thebes, for to live in the kingdom means to live in proper relationship with the members of the kingdom. Oedipus was in proper relationship with no one: he was the husband of his mother; he was the murderer of his father. And yet if anyone had asked Oedipus whether or not he lived in the kingdom of Thebes, he would think the questioner insane, for where else could he be?

We too regard ourselves as living on Earth. But we do not live on Earth in the sense of living as members of Earth's Community. We are simply not members so much as we are the unconscious destroyers of Earth's life.

We can't, with a single command, halt the destruction of the soils and the animals and the children, but we can with a single decision begin the search for ways to align our energies with the creative, restorative, and healing movements already taking place. In terms of our children, we can't instantly transform their education from industrial to Ecozoic (by "Ecozoic," I mean a form of education that would initiate our children into the ways of the universe). We can't instantaneously wash out all the trivialities and toxins and provide instead the knowledge and information essential for their future and the future of the planet. But we can begin to make a difference. We can begin by introducing our children and ourselves to the universe. We can start by showing our children they are part of a Big Picture; they have a place and a role in it. In time, if they are fortunate, they will learn to regard all the things of the world, even the briefest breath of the tiniest gnat, as woven into a single, comprehensive, coherent whole.

Here's a way to make a beginning. Get someone to show you where the constellation Sagittarius is, and then take a child outside and with that child direct your attention there. When you do so, you will be gazing into the very center of the Milky Way Galaxy, the hub around which all its three hundred billion stars revolve. By introducing young people to our galaxy as a whole and by allowing them the opportunity to understand themselves as living beings within this enveloping galactic process, they begin the deep journey into a much vaster context in which they can find the true meaning of their lives. Knowing the sacred direction toward the center of the galaxy and returning to it over and again will be part of the empowering process that will enable them, slowly and subconsciously, to think of themselves not just as political or economic entities. They will learn that they are, primarily, cosmological beings.

To speak in terms of light, we are twenty-five thousand light-years from the center of our Milky Way Galaxy. A light-year is a measurement of distance. It is the distance light will travel in a year's time, which is around 6 trillion miles. For instance, light from the center of the galaxy traveling 186,000 miles each second reaches us today after having streaked toward us for the last twenty-five thousand years. So if tonight you direct your gaze toward Sagittarius, some of the photons of light that reach you left the galactic center when giant woolly mammoths were roaming the North American continent.

The photons were created in those long-ago moments when Paleo-Indians revered and hunted these giant beasts. The saber-toothed tigers, like the Indians, stalked the mammoths and would continue to hunt another fifteen thousand years before disappearing in the amazing Quaternary extinction event. And in every instant of the saber-toothed tiger's existence, as generation after generation made its way, hunting and mating and sleeping and stalking, photons from the center of the galaxy were soaring silently through space on their journey toward Earth.

When a child looks toward the galactic center, she needs to remember the woolly mammoths and the saber-toothed tigers and the Paleo-Indians—and the brief period of time that has passed since civilization arose. All that great volume of time was necessary for the photons rushing at light speed to reach us tonight as we gaze into our galaxy's center.

Unless we live our lives with at least some cosmological awareness, we risk collapsing into miniscule worlds. We can be fooled into thinking that our lives are passed only in political entities, such as a state or a nation; or that the bottom-line concerns in life have to do only with economic realities. In truth, we live in the midst of immensities, and we are intrinsically woven into a great cosmic drama. Economic and political concerns are of real importance, but children need to understand that whatever significance and value these concerns have derive ultimately from our encompassing matrix and its deepest meanings. To be out of touch with this cosmological reality the reality in which we actually exist—is to risk living in a shrunken and distorted world, like Oedipus.

In addition to introducing our children to the center of the Milky Way Galaxy, we can orient them to something else, and that is Andromeda Galaxy. If we gaze toward the constellation also called Andromeda we will see there a faint blur of light unlike that of any of the stars. With an average pair of binoculars we can even see a spiral structure in the blur of light. This is the outer horizon of what the naked human eye can see, the light from Andromeda Galaxy, slightly larger than our Milky Way, coming to our eyes from 2.5 million light-years away.

Something happens in the soul of a child gazing at a blur of light while knowing this blur is a galaxy with hundreds of billions of stars. Something happens deep inside; a spaciousness opens up in psychic congruence with galactic spaciousness. That blur of light required millions of years to make it to this young human eye, and it is now an eye within a being who is aware of this. As the light enters in, her inner world opens out to a larger dimension.

On Earth 2.5 million years ago, humans were first discovering the use of tools, thereby entering into the long drama of seizing hold of the universe in a new way. On the day that early humans first started shaping human tools, light as always burst forth from Androm-eda, but this particular light had an extraordinary des-tiny, for as it streaked away from Andromeda and sped toward the Milky Way, inventive humans continued to develop their tools, their minds, their sensitivities, and their understanding, until at last, 2.5 million years later, they had come to comprehend their place the universe, just in time to take their children out to view the night sky, to let in and wonder over those same photons of light that had left their source so long ago. To gaze at Andromeda Galaxy is to enter into galactic spaciousness. It is to enter into a new sense of time. The human journey is as deep in time as the galaxies are distant in space.

Andromeda and the Milky Way are large galaxies, and they slowly pinwheel about each other. Each has a dozen or so galaxies encircling it. The best-known satellite galaxies circling the Milky Way are the Magellanic Clouds, Fornax, Draco, and Sculptor. Poor Andromeda has only very dull names—such as M32 for its companion galaxies. We have so little experience of them that we have not yet been able to name them properly. Before the twentieth century we didn't even know there were other galaxies in the universe, so naturally it is going to take some time before we move beyond just assigning numbers to galaxies.

The mega-system consisting of the Milky Way, Andromeda, and all of their satellite galaxies is spread out over several million light-years, contains at least half a trillion stars, and is called by astronomers the "Local Group." There's something both humorous and sad about that name, but we can consider it an interim tag, soon to be replaced by the names that poets of the twenty-first century invent as they learn this new story of the universe.

Our Local Group of galaxies itself is but one satellite of a still vaster system. Just as planet Earth revolves around the Sun, so too does our Local Group revolve around a central hub called the Virgo Cluster. Virgo, a gigantic cluster of three thousand galaxies, is fifty million light-years away. Our Local Group along with dozens of other galaxy clusters all revolve around the Virgo Cluster. When we reflect upon this entire supercluster system with its thousands upon thousands of galaxies, each of which might contain millions of exo-planets, the primate mind is dumbstruck. Just recently our major challenge was to grab hold of the next branch as we swung through the forests. Now we are left to ponder the immensities of this cluster of clusters, the Virgo Supercluster.

If we can now bring ourselves to imagine this immense supercluster as being a single white dot, then the universe as a whole consists of ten million of these that are floating, drifting, and twirling as apple blossoms do when in the early spring a gust of wind frees them from their branches and carries them aloft into the blue sky.

8

The Story Came to Us

Based on empirical evidence provided by the cosmic microwave background, the birth of the universe was 13.8 billion years ago. Concerning the overall size of the universe, calculations based on Einstein's general theory of relativity put the edge of the universe at 274 billion trillion miles away in space. These numbers have changed over the last century as instrumentation has improved, but exactitude is not the point here. What is astonishing is that scientists have discovered the birthplace of the empirically known universe.

When the astronomers Vesto Slipher, Edwin Hubble, and others first began gathering data on the motion of galaxies, they had no idea that they had embarked on an investigation that would lead to the discovery of the universe's birthplace. Indeed, few considerations could have been further from their minds. They were simply observing the universe and carefully attending to the movements of the galaxies.

It is significant that the very people who discovered the birthplace of the universe were shocked by the discovery. Some were depressed by it. Rather than trumpet their great achievement, they reported it with a sense of bafflement. Hubble, the scientist whose work was pivotal in convincing the scientific community that the universe had a birthplace, refused to provide interpretations. He simply published what he had found, however strange it might have appeared to him. And Einstein, whose theory provided the deepest interpretation of the data, began by actually altering some of his best ideas in order to avoid confronting their radical implications. At the very least we need to understand that the scientists were not projecting their mathematical theories or imposing their philosophical perspectives on the universe. They were observing the movements and structures in the universe. They were paying close attention to the patterns in the photons that came to them each night in their observatories.

The seemingly innocent phrase "came to them" hides yet another important truth that we need to bear in mind. Edwin Hubble and other scientists are members of the community of life on Earth, revolving around the Sun, in the three hundred billion stars of the Milky Way Galaxy, which pinwheels through our Local Group, all of it spinning inside the Virgo Supercluster, which dangles as one of ten million in the great universe. Scientists, and everyone else as well, can experience only what the universe brings to us here. What we know about the universe we have learned by listening to and reflecting on the news the universe brings.

As an illustration, we can return to our discussion of Andromeda Galaxy. Every night throughout all the millions of years of human existence, new photons of light have arrived from Andromeda. But it was not until we had painstakingly developed all the necessary tools, including telescopes and mathematics, but more generally all the arts and languages and conceptual capacities of modern *Homo sapiens*, that we could recognize the information these light particles carried. The story of Andromeda and its five hundred billion stars and its circling spiral structure has been present to Earth all along. And no one ever had to journey to Andromeda to learn its story. Rather, humans had to develop the sensitivities and capabilities necessary to awaken to the story that has been here throughout humanity's entire existence.

We scientists tend to use phrases that speak of our ability to "reach deep into space." We speak of our invention of instruments that "probe the farthest regions of the universe." These are certainly valid expressions, but they can also give the mistaken impression that we actually "reach out" in some literal sense. There is no reaching out. Rather, we reach into our immediate experience.

We reach into our experience of a small segment of the universe, and we find there photons with wondrous stories from the farthest regions of the universe. All the books on the distant galaxies, all the volumes and journal articles on the large-scale structure of the universe, all the tomes on the dynamics of neutron stars, all the photographs of the brilliant nebulae, all the studies of super red giants are, strictly speaking, explications of the stories that exist in each cubic centimeter of the universe. These stories have been there for all of human history, but not until recently have we been able to read them. Optical telescopes, infrared detectors, x-ray diffractometers, spectroscopic devices—all such instruments of modern astronomy are designed to decipher the news of the universe contained in each segment of it.

The discovery of the birthplace of the cosmos, then, is the discovery of the story that has been with us for millions of years. It showered us from all directions as we wandered the African savannas and built our mud abodes along the Nile. Our own generation is simply the one to emerge at the time when human consciousness has become subtle enough and complex enough to awaken to what the universe has been telling us from the beginning. If it is true that the discovery of the universe's birthplace is the work of a few spectacular geniuses, it is also true that the discovery is the work of the entire human venture. Every genius, even the greatest, comes out of and works within an understanding that has been developing over a hundred millennia. The deepening of mind necessary to hear the story of the universe required the complexification of consciousness coming from all two million years of the human journey since our discovery of tools.

We are the space the universe created in which to tell its stories.

9

Nighttime and Cosmic Rebirth

The more significant proposals humans make to one another often involve the light of the Moon. I wonder why this is so? After all, on a purely statistical basis, we live primarily in office buildings, traffic jams, dwellings, factories, and shopping malls.

It might have to do with courage. Sometimes it is hard to believe what we hear surging up from our hearts and we need to be half-hidden by the dark in order to blurt it out. Or perhaps we hear what is deepest in ourselves only in the dark. Perhaps night is a time when great discoveries are made because a beauty lives in the night that does not show itself at other times. However, the lesson of the night's sacred nature is so often forgotten. Immanuel Kant lamented our forgetting by claiming that, "If the stars came out once a century, humans would stay up all night long marveling at their beauty."

What about the day? The surprising thing is that the beauty is still there but hidden by another overpowering kind of beauty—the scattered blue light of day's sky. The stars shine always; they fill the skies both day and night. But night is a time free from daily scattered distractions. Night is a time when the presence of the stars can be more deeply felt, when the news of the universe can be more deeply attended to.

The ancient astronomers, the first cosmologists, and the shamanic storytellers often told their stories at night. The concerns of the day, however important they might seem in the sunlight, usually amount to nothing more than unwelcome distractions in the night when the great story is told in the glow from the fire's embers and in the white light of the Moon's journey through the branched shadows of the trees. It is in the peace that the night brings that something immense can stir in the depths of the listener, something not suspected during the day. Or if suspected briefly, then quickly forgotten as some daytime urgency presents itself. Late, very late, after the Sun has disappeared—such is the time for the great surprises deep in the listener's soul. Such is the time to ponder the mysteries of one's existence. What was invisible as we dashed about from one errand to another suddenly stands out, magically present and unavoidable.

As with so many epochal transformations of human consciousness, the discovery of the birthplace of the universe took place at night. It was a discovery that required the development of human intelligence over all two million years of human existence, a development that led to the capacity to be sensitive to and recognize the news the universe has been bringing to Earth. This sensitivity could be found in not just one particular human but in a small number of humans, including Hubble and Slipher, as well as Carl Wirtz, Howard Robertson, Willem de Sitter, and a few more. But, in a symbolic sense, I want to speak of the essential news as breaking forth in one particular human, as surfacing for the first time in the twentieth century's most celebrated scientist. To tell the story of the discovery of the birthplace of the universe is to tell the story of Albert Einstein.

The breakthrough moment occurred during the second decade of the twentieth century in Berlin. And although a novelist or a historian could perhaps detail in a straightforward manner the events that took place in that history-making time in Einstein's life, a cosmologist has a particular difficulty. My aim is to tell the story of the universe and, in speaking of Einstein, I am interested in him as one particular story within the encompassing story. So, in order to tell the story of Einstein I must first tell the story of the universe as a whole and then show how the story of Einstein fits into the encompassing story.

But here is the strange thing. How can I tell the story of the universe without first speaking of Einstein, through whose insight the story of the universe as a whole first started coming to light?

Einstein's theory can be seen as having a power that destroys one world and creates another. In approaching Einstein bent over his desk at night through the years of World War I, we see one event if we use the pre-Einsteinian physics of the modern period. But we see a larger and more inclusive Einstein-event if we use the physics that flowed from his pencil one particular night. He was, at that moment, literally destroying and then recasting a central code of Newtonian cosmology. In order, then, to understand what was happening there on the upper floor of a Berlin apartment, we need to understand that event through the very insights unfurling on the page.

No one in the entire world at that time could understand the reality of the Einstein-event. How could they? All had minds structured by one or more of the pre-Einsteinian cosmologies. In the West and in industrial countries generally, this would include the Newtonian worldview, a brilliant and profound system of concepts that had endured for three centuries, all the while guiding scientific research and offering a foundation for the authority of the social and political and economic structures congruent with that world of meaning.

Within the Newtonian framework the Einstein-event would be described along the following lines: "Albert Einstein, on November 22, 1914, articulated the gravitational dynamics of the universe in the form of his field equations." Or I could put it this way: "On November 22, 1914, Albert Einstein created his general theory of relativity, expanding his special theory of relativity to take into account gravitational effects." These sentences are true, but they miss in the grossest way the real drama taking place that night. To get a sense of what was actually happening we need to reflect on Einstein as he sat at his desk stunned by what had appeared on the paper.

To everyone alive at that time, his equation would appear to be just some letters and a few numbers scrawled onto the page. But to Einstein they revealed something unbelievable about the universe as a whole. Even though by this time he must have grown somewhat accustomed to the regularity with which shattering truths dropped from his fingertips, Einstein was stunned into bafflement by what he was seeing. Through these symbols, the universe whispered that it was expanding in all directions. No one in three centuries of modern scientific work had imagined such a possibility. All his life Einstein had assumed that the universe was an unchanging, infinite space. Now he was confronted with the idea that space was expanding in every direction. This was not a minor modification. This was an idea that, if true, would shatter the worldview of everyone, Einstein included.

Newton, Herschel, Galileo, Kepler, Darwin, Marie Curie, and all the scientists of the modern period took the universe to be an unchanging macrocosm. The universe was perceived as a vast and fixed place, a celestial container that housed the stars and planets and everything else. Then some strange symbols appeared, equations on the back of an envelope, mocking our former perspectives. A hieroglyphic arcanum in the language of differential geometry contained a bizarre truth that scientists would be unraveling for centuries: the universe had erupted fourteen billion years ago. The universe had a center—the place from which it emerged. The universe had an edge—the time at which it sprang forth.

Is it any wonder that Einstein rejected what his equations revealed? That he lost his nerve? That he altered them to hide their difficult truth? In all this, he was only too human, for how many of us are capable of accepting, all at once, the full truth when it comes in the form of a knife? How many of us let it cut through our hold on a false version of reality without first administering some edge-blunting that allows us to cling to one or two accustomed fictions?

Einstein doctored his equations. He added a mathematical term now known as the "cosmological constant." By altering the equations he took away their secret story of expansion and thereby preserved his attachment to an unchanging universe. It was only these altered equations that he published. Perhaps he was confident no one would notice. Perhaps he was hoping everyone would view the equations as another straightforward contribution to the scientific canon. But, as in those mythological stories where to change one word of a sacred chant is to throw the entire universe into chaos, so too with Einstein's sacred code.

Science is a collective enterprise. No genius, however magnificent, is sufficient alone to speak the truth. In Russia the mathematical cosmologist Alexander Friedmann, when pondering Einstein's equations, made what for him was a startling discovery. If one worked with these Einstein equations just a bit, dropping off this one strange term, why, it turned out that Einstein's equations pointed to an expanding universe!

Imagine Friedmann's excitement as he rushed to write a letter to Einstein to tell him of his discovery. I only wish someone had snapped a photograph of Einstein's face when he unfolded the letter from this excited young mathematician. Einstein thought he had put that business behind him, and now it was back, staring him in the face as he experienced the truth of a melancholy wisdom: "One finds one's destiny on the path one takes to avoid it."

As it turned out, Friedmann's work failed to convince Einstein. But in the next decade Edwin Hubble in California trained his telescope on distant galaxies and saw that they were in fact expanding away from us. Finally, when Hubble invited Einstein down to Mount Palomar to see for himself, Einstein accepted the fact that the old idea of the universe as a fixed, unchanging macrocosm, the notion of the universe as simply a giant box, was wrong. Only when Einstein saw with his own eyes the galaxies expanding away from us did he realize that his original insight concerning a dynamic, expanding universe had in fact been the truth.

The universe was evolving. The universe had an edge to its existence. The universe had a birthplace. All of this had been predicted by his original equations, but it had just been too much to absorb. The idea that the universe as a whole was expanding had completely dumbfounded the greatest scientist of the last thousand years.

10

The Place Where the Universe Began

If we look out beyond the Milky Way Galaxy and out beyond the Local Group of galaxies, if we look out into the great sea of galaxy clusters, we find that the clusters are moving away from us. This is true whether we look at the clusters that are straight above the Milky Way Galaxy or to the west, to the south, to the east, to the north, or down below the Milky Way. In every direction we look, we find the clusters of galaxies expanding away from us.

Reflecting on this bizarre discovery, the Belgian scientist Georges Lemaître hypothesized that the universe as a whole must have begun as a point that exploded in a titanic burst of energy. Not only are the galaxies expanding away from each other, they are moving away with a velocity related to the space between them. *The farther apart they are, the faster they are flying away from each other.* More precisely: galaxies twice as far apart are sailing away from each other twice as fast. Galaxies ten times as far apart are sailing away ten times as fast.

The mathematical conclusion could not be more startling: by tracing the trajectories of the superclusters of galaxies backward, we find an event of cataclysmic energy where all trillion galaxies are brought into a single ineffable point, the birthplace of the universe, the initial singularity of space-time, the center of the universe. There, in that place, the entire cosmos began as a pinprick, a sextillion-ton pinprick layered with the power to thunder forth into the beauty of existence.

This vast and complex tapestry of being—the Magellanic Clouds, the Milky Way, Andromeda, the many thousands of shining spirals and ellipticals of the Virgo Supercluster of galaxies—all of these are sailing off from an initial birthplace. And each supercluster rushes away from every other supercluster, all of them emerging from a single point.

The idea that the universe began in one place is certainly an ancient one in human history. The notion of a birthplace of the universe occurs in the mythical and classical forms of consciousness, and possibly even earlier. Such images as "the cosmic egg" that cracks open and gives birth to all phenomena are found in Neolithic cultures around the planet. Thus, the scientific discovery has the dual nature of being both old and new simultaneously. The mathematical theories and observational data are indeed new, and they represent a new kind of knowing; yet the overarching images are very old.

We need continually to distinguish the scientific enterprise from earlier forms of inquiry in order to avoid the two most common errors: insisting that scientific understanding is altogether divorced from other kinds of knowing, or claiming that in essence there is no difference between the modern scientific and the other forms of knowledge. Each mode is primordial; each is qualitatively distinct from the others. Science is an investigation of the universe rooted in empirically verifiable physical detail and is complementary to our earlier and more intuitive investigations of reality. The aim is not to eliminate one way of knowing in favor of the other; the aim in an ultimate sense is an integral understanding of the universe grounded both in scientific empirical detail and in our primordial poetic visions of the cosmos.

One of the principal differences in these approaches is the scientific hypothesis. Science does not proceed from one well-established fact to the next. Instead, science proceeds with a series of hypotheses that can be tested and confirmed or rejected on the basis of empirical discoveries. Science then offers a hypothetical story of reality that is constantly being revised, but that is stronger and more dependable with each generation for the simple reason that an ever larger body of data is appropriated into its intellectual framework.

Lemaître's theory that the universe began in a great explosion offers a clear example of how science arrives at knowledge. When Lemaître initially postulated his theory, it was just one among several different theories about the universe and its development. Each of these theories accounted for the facts of the universe that we knew, but each also made predictions about the facts of the universe we would discover in the future. Lemaître's hypothesis of a fiery beginning slowly advanced in status from postulate to scientific knowledge when in 1964 Arno Penzias and Robert Wilson detected the light left over from the explosion that Lemaître had postulated. Penzias and Wilson captured the photons—the particles of light—that had been set in motion fourteen billion years ago when the universe erupted into existence.

This discovery opens the door to another trajectory into the meaning of the sentence, "The birthplace of the universe can be found by tracing back to the origin the photons of light that erupted at the birthplace of the universe."

The light Penzias and Wilson discovered originated in the primeval fireball itself, and had been traveling for fourteen billion years. To trace these photons back is to follow the trail to that sacred place where the universe first flared forth into existence. That place from which the photons left is the cosmic center, the world's navel, the sacred origin point of being. It is the place endowed with the stupendous fecundity necessary to give birth to the cosmos.

Whereas former mythical consciousness might have created images of our cosmic birth, and whereas classical consciousness might have reasoned philosophically and theologically about the universe's beginning, scientific consciousness has located in an empirical way the physical birthplace of the universe. I neither want to claim that scientists were the first to discover the story—obviously humans had for millennia spoken in various languages about the birth of the universe—nor do I want to pretend that science is only corroborating what earlier people already knew—we now have some details of the story that were never even suspected in earlier times. Instead, I want to remember that humans have a variety of paths to the truth, and that when these various routes arrive at a common consensual knowledge, we have the possibility of a story of the universe that can guide us as a whole species in this new millennium.

If the news from science consisted solely of this fact that the birthplace of the universe could be gotten to by tracing the path of the primordial photons back to their birthplace, we would already have a magnificent new understanding of the universe, for now we would have discovered the actual place of its origin. But the story has one added complexity. In order to achieve a fuller understanding, we need to move beyond a paradox that I have avoided mentioning explicitly but that is most likely hunkered down in the basement of your mind, with the apparent irrationality of that paradox sapping your psychic energy.

11

A Multiplicity of Centers

I stated earlier that when Edwin Hubble began looking at the galaxies, he discovered that the galaxy clusters were moving away from us in all directions. What I did not point out then is the startling conclusion that, in terms of cosmic expansion, we *find ourselves at the center of the cosmos*. This is indeed a strange and most unexpected development.

If such a discovery had been made during the medieval period in Europe it would have caused no surprise at all, for the prevailing worldview at that time put the Earth at the center of the universe. To extend Earth's centrality to the center of expansion of all the galaxy clusters would have made no great demands on the medieval mind.

But, of course, at the time Hubble made his discovery we no longer had a medieval worldview. We had already learned from Copernicus that Earth is not a fixed point at the center of the universe. Earth is one planet moving around one star, which itself is one of the three hundred billion stars of the Milky Way Galaxy, which in turn is one of a trillion galaxies in the vast universe. If we have learned anything over the last four hundred years since Copernicus initiated this great search, we have certainly learned that Earth is not a fixed center around which all the planets and stars revolve.

And yet, here is this new revelation placing us at the center of the cosmic expansion of the galaxy clusters. Our Virgo Supercluster is not moving at all, and all of the other superclusters are moving away from us. What are we supposed to make of it?

Complicating our challenge is the consternation of the scientists who discovered the expansion. If we could convince ourselves that it was Einstein's secret hope to put us at the center of the universe, we could dismiss his work and that of others doing similar work as an attempt to impose an ideological framework on the universe. On the contrary, as we have already seen explicitly in Einstein's case and as was the case with other scientists as well, the very discoverers of the cosmic expansion were repulsed by what they had discovered, and they did everything they could to avoid accepting it.

Had the cultural and personal biases of these scientists determined what they saw, they would not have found all the clusters of galaxies moving away from us so symmetrically that we were placed at the very center of this cosmic expansion. If they had been free to distort the data to fit their own preconceived notions about the large-scale nature of the universe, they would have announced that all the galaxies were fixed with respect to each other, which is what Einstein's doctored equations suggested. Or, if they couldn't have an unchanging universe, they might have preferred one in which all the galaxies were moving in the same direction, a Great River of galaxies. Then at least we would not be in any special place. Such a discovery would thus fit smoothly into modern culture, for it would suggest we were insignificant, without cosmic meaning, just as Friedrich Nietzsche and Jean-Paul Sartre and Bertrand Russell and so many other modern philosophers were teaching. Earth would be just one bit of bark being swept along in the Great Current.

What Hubble discovered did not fit our modern culture's preconceptions—it disrupted them. But instead of altering his data, he published it. He offered no philosophical comment on the data. He simply reported his results. In terms of the universe as a whole, we find ourselves at the center of a fourteen-billion-year expansion.

Hubble's discovery is the completion of the cosmological exploration that Copernicus began. Copernicus initiated an investigation that led to the removal of the Earth from the center of the universe, then removed the Sun from the center, and then removed everything from the center. But after four hundred years of empirical inquiry, a great reversal has taken place, one that shows us to be at the center of a universe vastly huger than the solar system and nearby stars that Copernicus and Galileo were aware of. We do not return to the cozy medieval geocentric world but instead enter an immense evolutionary cosmos, a cosmos that is centered on its own expansion. In order to fully appreciate this new understanding of the cosmic center we must now deal with the seeming paradox at the heart of the data.

I've presented two discoveries that seem in conflict with each other. First, in terms of the light from the beginning of time, which was first detected by Penzias and Wilson, the birthplace of the universe is fourteen billion light-years away from us. Second, in terms of the expansion of the galaxies, which is Hubble's discovery, we are at the very center of the universe. We need to consider this strange situation in which we are simultaneously at the center of the cosmic expansion and fourteen billion light-years away from it. How can we be both at the center, and fourteen billion light years away from the center?

We have difficulties with the apparent contradiction in these discoveries because our minds have been shaped and educated in a culture firmly rooted in the Newtonian worldview. Even though we now know Newtonian physics is not adequate for understanding the vast evolutionary universe that has been discovered since Newton's death, we are nevertheless stuck with Newtonian consciousness because it forms the foundation of our major institutions—including our educational systems. The challenge of understanding an Einsteinian universe is a real challenge indeed. We need to reinvent our very minds so that we do not distort the discoveries by placing them into Newtonian categories that are unable to contain the truths we have discovered.

A single example can help clarify this discussion of centers. When we hear that the universe began in a great explosion fourteen billion years ago, we picture this as something like a Fourth of July fireworks explosion. First there is just empty space, then there's this great burst of colors in all directions. We are forced into picturing the birth of the universe in this way because Newtonian cosmology regarded the universe as a giant fixed space inside of which things move about and gather together and so forth. The shaping of our minds in childhood already compels us to picture the birth of the universe as an explosion taking place in an already existing space.

But this understanding of the universe's beginning is both false and utterly misleading. The birth of the universe means not only the birth of all the elementary particles of the universe and not only the birth of all the light and energy of the universe, it also means *the birth of the space and time of the universe*. There is no pre-existing Newtonian space into which the universe explodes. There is no external Newtonian timepiece ticking away outside the universe. Space and time emerge together with mass and energy in the primordial mystery of the universe's flaring forth.

The simplest way of seeing the inadequacy of our mind's Newtonian assumptions concerning the universe's beginning is to ask a simple question. When I picture the cosmic birth as some kind of explosion that is taking place off in the distance, away from me, away from where I am observing it, just where am I standing?

What provides the platform for my feet? How is it that I can stand outside the universe and watch its birth if I myself, from the beginning, am woven into this birth?

A re-education of the mind is necessary to make sense of what we have discovered. The central archetypal pattern for understanding the nature of the universe's birth and development is omnicentricity. The large-scale structure of the universe is qualitatively more complex than either the geocentric picture of medieval cultures or the fixed Newtonian space of modern culture. What we have discovered is an omnicentric evolutionary universe, a developing reality which from the beginning is centered upon itself at each place of its existence. In this universe of ours, to be in existence is to be at the cosmic center of the complexifying whole.

If there are Hubble-like beings in the Hercules Cluster of galaxies seven hundred million light-years away, and if such creatures are pondering the universe from that perspective, they will also discover that the galaxies in the universe are moving away from them. They will thus conclude on the basis of this evidence that they are at the center of the universe's expansion, and they will be correct. Our Newtonian minds might experience discomfort in trying to grasp this, but our personal difficulties do not change the nature of the universe. Just as Einstein's first reaction when he was given a glimpse of our omnicentric evolutionary cosmos was to pull back and insist that the universe could not be like that, so too in our own struggle we sometimes wish that the universe were not so complex, not so mysterious. But the universe will be what it will be regardless of whether or not we humans accept it as it is.

There is one image in the scientific literature that can assist us in our attempt to understand a universe that is omnicentric. I offer this image with some misgivings because, however helpful it may be in some ways, it is also inadequate in others, as I will point out. My hope is that it can help us take a first step out of the false view of the universe as a fixed space. And perhaps it might help awaken more adequate images of the nature of the universe that will become a regular part of our cosmological education in the future.

Imagine you are inside a rising loaf of raisin bread. The crucial point is to begin this work of imagination from within the process rather than outside of it. So you have to forget the nagging Newtonian questions concerning the edge of the loaf or any other concern that arises when you attempt to understand the process from *outside*. Even your thoughts about this process are simply an interesting current of micro-events taking place inside the great macro-event of the rising loaf.

In this particular raisin bread image you need to focus your imagination totally on being inside the leavened raisin bread. Imagine yourself sitting on a raisin and looking around. You will see that all the other raisins are moving away from you as the bread expands, so that you find yourself at the very center. And anyone else on any other raisin throughout the loaf will come to a similar conclusion—hence, we have in this raisin loaf a model for an omnicentric reality.

But there's more. Suppose you now try to determine whether or not you and your raisin are moving with respect to the bread itself. What you will find of course is that you're frozen in place, for your raisin sits *stationary* with respect to the surrounding bread. And when you think about it a bit you realize that the very reason the raisins are moving away from you is the *expansion* of the bread. You and your raisin are not even moving; it's the space in between the raisins that is growing larger as the yeast releases carbon dioxide gas.

And that, precisely, is how we understand the cosmic expansion. It is not the movement of galaxies through an already existing, fixed, Newtonian space. No, it's much more interesting than that. The cause of the expansion of the universe is the space emerging into existence and pushing the clusters apart from each other. The size of each galaxy cluster stays the same, but the space *in between* the clusters expands in each instant, which results in an ever larger universe. That is our new understanding of the cosmos as a whole. A wild spirit breathes forth space that explodes the primeval fireball into a great billowing immensity at whose center we find ourselves.

In terms of the large-scale expansion of the universe, we are not moving. We are at the stable and unmoving center of this expansion. To be in the universe is to be at its center.

We are now in a position to show how the seeming paradox of being at the center and 274 billion trillion miles from the center is in fact simply a counterintuitive feature of existence within an expanding universe. To see this, imagine we are back near the beginning of time; in fact, imagine we are right at the moment when the fireball begins to break apart and release its light in all directions.

Now, let's follow the adventure of a particle of light that is released very near to us. *If the universe were not expanding*, such a particle of light would fly across the distance separating us in an instant. But since the universe is not just expanding, but is expanding extremely rapidly, the particle of light has to travel a much greater distance as time passes. It's as if we were waiting at the top of the "down" escalator, and someone on the second step wants to reach us. The escalator begins moving very rapidly downward so that our friend, whose velocity never varies, is at first carried away from us. But as time passes the escalator begins to slow down so that eventually our friend makes it all the way back up the stairs and joins us at the top.

Just this happened with the photons of light released in the early moments of the universe's existence. Those photons that were traveling in our direction were carried away from us by the rapid expansion of the universe. But as with a ball thrown up toward the sky whose initial speed upward slows down with every passing second, so too with the expansion of the universe, which began very rapidly but then began to slow down as gravity worked against it. Those photons that were initially carried away from us kept traveling in our direction and eventually completed the journey to us.

The photons of light that arrived here in 1964 (and were detected by Penzias and Wilson) had been traveling toward us for fourteen billion years. So we can say that their place of origin is *now* 274 billion trillion miles away from us. On the other hand, if we go back in time, we find that their place of origin *back then* is very close to where we are now.

I know what you are thinking. That it's all too complicated to understand. But the truth is, the complication comes from our assumption that the birth of the universe takes place in a pre-existing space. That is how Newton thought, and we have been socialized into thinking that way—that space as an extremely large, empty room. But Einstein has gone beyond that. The universe began smaller than an acorn and space emerged *inside* the acorn. That is the discovery of Einstein, Lemaître, Hubble, Penzias, and Wilson. Something smaller than an acorn expanded into two trillion galaxies.

Like every other point in the universe, our own place here on Earth in the Virgo Supercluster is an origin point of the universe. The matter we are composed of stayed *here* as the primordial light emanated away from us fourteen billion years ago. If there are intelligent beings elsewhere in the universe, they may be detecting those very photons of light that left from here and that now arrive in their own distant planetary system. Such photons will carry news of *our place* as the origin of the light from the beginning of time. We exist then at the origin point of the universe, because every place in the universe is that place where the universe flared forth into existence.

12

Cosmic Desire

I now make a shift in our discussion. I have been carefully relaying the fundamental contours of our current understanding of the universe as a whole. My presentation has been guided by the astounding discoveries of a fourteen-billion-year evolutionary process. These discoveries have been widely accepted as scientific facts. For the remaining chapters, although I will continue to draw upon the sciences of quantum physics and mathematical cosmology, I will also include speculations on the universe, speculations, intuitions, and hypotheses that move beyond established scientific fact. All of these intuitions seem entirely reasonable extensions from the science to the speculative cosmology, but some may seem off to you. You may have a qualitatively different way of interpreting the data. To keep things straight, think of the preceding chapters as a scientific explication of the omnicentric universe based on Einstein's equations and Hubble's observations. What follows is my reflection upon these discoveries, a modest contribution to philosophical cosmology that could be called, to distinguish it from the science, the philosophical doctrine of "omnicentrism."

As I indicated in a previous chapter, this book belongs to, and carries forward, the cosmological lineage—a scientific, literary, and oral art form found among humans everywhere on the planet. As an enterprise, cosmology began when people gathered together in the dark and told their stories of the universe. It is quite possible that the very first works of cosmology emerged three hundred thousand years ago with the birth of *Homo sapiens*.

Though the majority of these cosmological stories are probably lost forever, I want to focus on two stories here: humanity's earliest cosmology, and our most recent cosmological narrative. My philosophical assumption is that both of these cosmologies have value, as do all of the cosmologies that come between them. In constructing our new cosmology of the twenty-first century, we need to draw upon the wealth of previous attempts by our ancestors.

We begin with the culture of the !Kung Bushmen, one of the oldest on Earth, who tell stories of Kaang, the Great Lord of All Life. Kaang began by creating a huge tree that covered the world. At the bottom of the tree trunk he dug a hole, out of which the first man and the first woman and then all the animals emerged.

The most recent cosmology is that of the Modern World, which has produced the narrative that starts with the Big Bang and marches forward from the simplest beginnings to the complex world of today. Elementary particles joined together to form the nuclei of various light elements such as hydrogen, helium, and lithium. As the universe expanded and cooled, the first atoms were drawn together by the gravitational attraction of baryonic (ordinary) matter and dark matter into the stars and galaxies. Some of the early stars ended in a violent explosion out of which all of the heavy elements were synthesized, everything from beryllium to carbon to uranium. On a rocky planet, chemical reactions brought forth cellular life. These primal organisms gradually became involved with one another in an ongoing synthesis that led to the organic evolution of sponges, echinoderms, flowers, and diverse plants and animals, including a seventy-million-year primate lineage leading to the self-reflexive consciousness of *Homo sapiens*, such as the !Kung Bushmen and Modern Humans.

For the !Kung, the power that makes things happen is named Kaang. For Moderns, the powers that make things happen are named Gravity, Electromagnetism, the Second Law of Thermodynamics, and Natural Selection. For my omnicentric worldview, I want to bring these into a new conception of "universe." Throughout the modern period, the word "universe" has meant "everything that is." The universe consists of galaxies with stars and planets and all sorts of living and non-living entities. Things happen all the time. Clouds of hydrogen collapse down to a star because the gravitational interaction is drawing the matter to a center.

The one small change in modern cosmology that I want to introduce is to say that when gravity is at work, the universe is acting. Gravity and the other physical processes are what the universe does. It is the universe that is drawing astronomical bodies toward each other. On one level, linguistically, this is easy to adjust to. When lightning strikes, we can say, "The universe has generated lightning." Or when considering how a species of life evolved through the processes of natural selection and genetic mutation, we can say, "The universe created a new species." All these physical processes are part of the universe, so when they happen, it is the universe happening.

The challenge posed by this idea of the universe acting through physical interactions has to do with intention. It comes down to a simple question. Does the universe just happen? Or does the universe intend to bring electrons together with protons to form hydrogen? This can be expressed in terms of !Kung cosmology by asking, "Is the universe like Kaang? Does it have desires and intentions like Kaang, or like a human being, or like an animal or a plant?"

Throughout the four hundred years of modern science, educated people took it for granted that the universe did not have intention. The universe was a vast conglomeration of entities and processes. There was no Kaang directing things. Things just were the way they were. All entities were made of atoms, and these atoms were controlled by mathematical laws as discovered by Isaac Newton and James Clerk Maxwell and Albert Einstein. That was the modern mechanical view of the universe, and it remains the dominant view of the universe in industrial societies.

The difference today is that we need to take into account science's amazing discoveries, beginning with cosmic evolution. We now know that our universe evolved from a simple plasma to galaxies with living planets. What baffles us is the rapidity with which this happened. There was no outside force that brought forth complexity. It was simply the universe with its physical interactions, but these physical interactions surprise us with their rush to bring forth structure, life, and mind. Before we discovered cosmic evolution, the strengths of the various physical interactions were understood to be absurd, in the sense of without meaning. They just were what they were. The strong nuclear interaction holding together the protons in a nucleus just was what it was. There was no meaning in the size of that strength. The size was without relevance to the universe as a whole.

This view has turned out to be completely wrong. In a series of stunning discoveries, physicists have come to understand that the physical processes taking place in the original fireball at the beginning of time possessed a power and an order that pertained to events billions of years in the future. The strong nuclear interaction between two protons was precisely what it had to be in order for long-burning stars to appear. If the strength were altered by as little 2 percent, the entire future existence of life in the universe would never have been possible. I'm not sure what language will be used by twenty-second-century scientists to refer to this discovery, but I am quite confident that our descendants will abandon the idea that the physical processes are absurd, or irrational, or meaningless. We have discovered an order inside the earliest moments of the primordial fireball that demands to be included in our new cosmology.

How are we to speak of this elegant order involving the strong nuclear interaction?

One thing that is very clear is that the universe is not entirely random. If the universe were random, there would be no preferred directions for the universe to move in. But even from the earliest moments, the universe is moving toward the construction of stars. We can summarize this situation by saying that the universe has *inclinations* to move in certain directions. Or we can say that the universe has fundamental preferences for its movements. Our universe is not indifferent. It is not pure chaos. The universe has inclinations and preferences for its ongoing unfolding.

I speak of this inclination in the universe as being a desire, or an urge. I do not mean "desire" the way a human feels desire, or the way a mammal feels desire. The word is used as an analogy. It is used to point to a dynamic in the universe that is analogous to human desire. One of the best illustrations of this can be found in the first instants of time, when the universe-plasma consisted of matter and light and had a temperature of a trillion degrees. The stable structures of atoms were not possible, even though the strong nuclear and the electromagnetic interactions were at work. The universe was too dense for any structures to form. A thimbleful of the primordial fireball weighed billions of tons and was exploding with energy. Its power was uncontainable, its expansion unstoppable. As it spread out and cooled, it revealed the order inherent in its processes. It has harbored that order since the beginning of time. When the right moment arrives, first atoms and eventually galaxies come forth. Atoms and the galaxies are the expressions of the universe's aim. The primordial fireball expanded even faster than the speed of light to get to the point at which it could form billions of galaxies. That was the aim it carried in the mathematical order of its physical processes. Given its density, given the elegance of its physical interactions and its temperature, the primeval fireball had a pathway into the future that was ineluctable. It would become a billion galaxies. The primordial desire of the universe would be inexorable.

13
Universe Guidance

Will the new cosmology alter the way we feel about our existence?

A personal story. In 1987, I was asked to address a group of Christian ministers in Burlingame, California. I had recently published a book on the evolutionary universe and I was soaring with enthusiasm. My audience was a small group, maybe eighty people. Because I'm six foot five, I naturally tend to focus my attention on the back of the room and don't notice the first couple of rows when I speak. So there I was, overflowing with ideas, getting more and more excited as I told them how vast the universe was, how many billions of galaxies it contained, how many hundreds of billions of stars have come and gone over the ages, and so forth.

At some point I heard what sounded like muffled sobs. When I looked down, to my astonishment, I saw that a woman in the first row was weeping. Her eyes were puffy under her glasses, which suggested she'd been at it for a while. With great alarm in my voice, I asked her what the matter was.

She looked up at me. "Why do you want to destroy me?"

It was a decisive moment in my life. I had been trying to share my excitement about the universe and I ended up inflicting only confusion and misery on her. It was entirely my fault. I had not yet recognized the necessity of reflecting on the relationship of the individual to the whole.

Our understanding of the universe will affect in deep ways how we feel about our existence, what we regard as important. Any change in our fundamental cosmology will ripple out into our emotions and our deepest values. The relationships intrinsic to an omnicentric universe are qualitatively different from the relationships that characterize the modern industrial era, as can be seen quickly by examining the thought of any of the major thinkers. René Descartes, for instance, held that matter was just inert stuff, and that even animals were nothing more than machines. Descartes did not know that this inert matter and these animal-machines were his progenitors. Thus it was that with innocent ignorance he gave birth to an ideal philosophy for constructing a planet-wide consumerism.

The radical transformation that follows from our understanding of an omnicentric universe can be stated in a single line: *the universe focuses on its parts*. I gave one example of this in the previous chapter when I spoke of the universe's inclination to bring forth galaxies. This inclination does not end with galaxies but carries on through billions of years. The universe aims at stars, the universe aims at planets, the universe aims at life, in the sense that if the fundamental dynamics at work in the fireball had been different in even the smallest way, there would be no stars, no planets, no life. There is also chance involved in the process. The primordial fireball would bring forth galaxies, of that there is no doubt. But that the specific Andromeda Galaxy would emerge is a surprise that comes out of the blizzard of chance interactions through time. Neither the whole nor the part is the ultimate reality. It is the ongoing interactions between the whole and its parts that determine the specific facets of the universe.

The main psychological obstacle preventing entrance into experiencing the omnicentric universe is the Newtonian notion of space as a giant, empty room. This conception is dominant throughout industrial societies today and makes impossible any significant discussion of the dynamic relationships tying parts and whole together, other than to say that the parts relate to the universe like aluminum chairs relate to an empty auditorium. So long as the notion of a passive universe has a hold on our minds, we will fail to appreciate that reality comes forth out of the ongoing, dynamic, and creative relationships between whole and parts.

As a way of breaking out of this view of things, we can take advantage of the central ideas of Einstein's special theory of relativity. Einstein is universally regarded as one of the greatest geniuses of the last thousand years because of the way in which his work shattered Newton's notion that the universe is passive and that time is universal. Though every university today teaches Einstein's theories, we are a long way from absorbing the implications of his thought into our lived reality. Most of us continue to think that there is one timepiece somewhere keeping track of the passage of time. However, according to Einstein's special theory of relativity, the time of each entity in the universe is uniquely its own. To be precise, if I am in motion relative to you, my time will slow down. Even if we have identical timepieces, even if they are the most accurate in the world, my time will be slowed down compared to yours. The point I wish to emphasize here is that the actual time in which you live is unique to you. As surprising as this might sound, such is a central insight of Einstein's theory.

In practical terms, if the speed of my motion is small, the difference between my time and yours is negligible. The difference does not show itself in a palpable way until the relative velocity of two people approaches the speed of light. But the size of the differences in the sense of time between two people or two animals on Earth is not the point. *The amazing fact is that each entity has its own time.* This assertion of Einstein has been checked many thousands of times. It is one of the most tested theories in the history of science. I have focused here on time, but the same can be said for space. Namely, each entity in the universe lives in its own space, where its measurements of things will be uniquely its own. As before, the discrepancies between spatial measurements made by two people on Earth will be extremely small, but they will be real. Einstein's theory of the relativity of space and time is a shocking demolition of Newton's theory of absolute space and time. Dwell a moment on what this means. The universe is not passive. The universe centers itself on you in that all the objects you see around you are experienced in a way unique to you. In a manner that stuns our modern minds, the universe, moment by moment, is organizing itself so that our experiences are unique.

All I have presented thus far concerning Einstein's theory is straight science. Now I will offer my own speculation as to how the special theory of relativity might be the first glimmer of a much deeper understanding of the universe's dynamism that our descendants will articulate in greater detail.

To say that the early universe inclines towards galaxies is equivalent to saying that the universe aims at becoming itself. Every entity desires to bring forth its latency, to give it form, to release it into the adventure of cosmic evolution. The relationship between part and whole has to do with the fulfillment that comes with creativity. The part desires to give expression to its depths, and the whole organizes itself with respect to that. The primordial fireball yearns to bring forth galaxies, and the universe spreads matter out and combines it gravitationally so that this can happen.

My speculation concerning every entity, including human beings, is that the universe is organizing itself to empower the unique development of each being. Fix this idea in your mind by considering the situation of a cloud of hydrogen drifting about in the Milky Way Galaxy. Latent in this cloud is an unborn star. The cloud by itself cannot bring forth this star. If it were left to itself, it would drift about for a trillion years without any substantial change. But it is not isolated; it is contained in a whole called the Milky Way Galaxy, which has density waves sweeping through the entire disk of stars and gases that can ignite the star. I summarize this by saying that Einstein's equations help us see how the whole of the galaxy is organizing itself in order to empower the unique development of its clouds of hydrogen and helium. The science is clear and is restricted to physical interactions. But perhaps over time we will learn that there are subtle dimensions of this process that escape easy detection.

My speculation is that, in the future, scientists will learn how the universe, and the galaxy, organize our worlds so that we might discover our destiny within the great drama of Earth's life. This insight concerning the universe has been intuited since ancient times, as when ancestors saw in the flight of birds, or in the sudden onset of a storm, significant signposts for how they should live. The universe offered insights into pathways they might take to find their unique fulfillment.

An omnicentric universe is filled with voices calling us into deep activation. When we find our way into alignment, the energy that constructed the galaxies flows in our veins. We were a part, now we are whole. Our fulfillment is to become the heart of the universe in the form of a human being.

14

The Origin

We have one last question to explore: "If the universe began fourteen billion years ago in a blast of energy, what is the nature of our origin?" In seeking out the answer to this question we need to complete our journey to the heart of the universe by approaching the power that gave birth there at the center of things.

The discovery that we exist at the birthplace of the universe is monumental. It amounts to a cultural announcement that humanity is in the midst of a move to a new cosmological understanding of itself. But even as we are astounded by the truth of omnicentricity, we need to approach a discovery that is as difficult to absorb as the omnicentric nature of the universe.

It helps to keep Einstein in mind. If someone with such extraordinary conceptual powers had difficulty appropriating the new story of the universe, we can expect to experience a certain amount of consternation as we struggle to acquire understanding. The emergence of novel truths concerning cosmological questions brings both fear and joy. Intense emotional reactions are inevitable, for there is no easy way to accept a re-envisioning of the universe in its most basic dimensions. I invoke the genius of Einstein once again as we confront one last twentieth-century discovery, that of the quantum vacuum.

As I have said earlier, one of the principal difficulties in understanding the new story is the Newtonian cast of our minds. This is nowhere more true than in the way we understand "the vacuum." For the modern mind, "the vacuum" means empty space. It means nothingness. It means "naught." And while there is a way in which such definitions can be considered true, we have discovered a deeper and more subtle dimension to the vacuum that we need to explore here.

Scientific discussions concerning the vacuum sometimes point to the regions between the superclusters as the best approximation to a pure vacuum, since matter and energy are truly rare in these regions. This is a reasonable way to proceed so long as we remember that the vacuum is everywhere. It is what we are left with when all entities are removed. Once all the atoms and molecules and particles and quanta have been taken out of a place, all that remains is "vacuum," or "quantum field."

Now for the news: careful investigation of this vacuum by quantum physicists reveals the strange appearance of elementary particles out of this emptiness. Even where there are no atoms, and no elementary particles, and no protons, and no photons, suddenly elementary particles will emerge. Quanta simply foam into existence.

I understand how bizarre and far-fetched this might sound for anyone learning it for the first time. But there is simply no way to make this discovery "reasonable." Most of us have Newtonian minds with a built-in prejudice that thinks of the vacuum as dead. If we insist that only material is real and that the vacuum is dead and inert, we will have to find some way to keep ourselves ignorant of this deep discovery by physicists: *elementary particles emerge from the "vacuum."* They do not sneak in from some hiding place when we are not looking. Nor are they bits of light transformed into protons. These elementary particles crop up out of the vacuum itself— that is the simple and awesome discovery I keep repeating myself, because even though I have known this for decades, the truth of it continues to amaze me. I am asking you to contemplate a universe where being arises out of a field of "fecund emptiness."

The emergence of protons and anti-neutrons out of a quantum field is not some unusual event taking place off in the regions between the superclusters of galaxies. This radical emergence takes place everywhere and at all times. The reason it has taken us so many millennia to discover this process is its subtlety. It takes place in a realm our eyes cannot detect. The usual process is for particles to erupt in pairs that will quickly interact and annihilate each other. Electrons and positrons, protons and anti-protons, all of these are suddenly appearing, and just as quickly vanishing again, throughout the universe.

Before we go further into this discussion, I want to stop a moment and reflect briefly on two of the reasons why this discovery will be especially difficult for us modern and postmodern people to comprehend. The first difficulty is linguistic, the second philosophical.

"Vacuum" as a word is truly pathetic as a term for what we are discussing here. At least in the English language, "vacuum" makes us think of a small, squarish device with hoses that is especially good for sucking up gum wrappers underneath our car seats. There's something terribly wrong about using a word with such homely connotations to refer to the basal generative power of the universe. I have suggestions for replacements, but before we discuss those, let's consider the second, philosophical difficulty.

A significant part of our modern, industrial consciousness is based on the philosophical assumption that "reality" means "material things." We further assume, usually unconsciously, that the "really real" of any entity is its material components. The *whole* is seen as flimsy and derivative; the part as sturdy and primary. This reductionistic materialism is an outgrowth of a scientific tradition that held that the universe was built out of indestructible atoms, a tradition going back at least to Democritus in the classical Greek world. Certainly scientific understanding has benefited tremendously from this tradition. Because of it we were led to determine how every object in the universe is indeed composed of atoms. This was far from obvious for earlier investigators and was in fact bitterly contested until it was empirically demonstrated in the nineteenth and early twentieth centuries. To discover that cumulus clouds, the Sun, and an ostrich are all composed of the same atomic elements is undoubtedly one of the greatest achievements of the human venture, and the atomic theory of matter is without question among the most robust in all of contemporary science.

The difficulty begins when we jump to the further philosophical assumption that reality is identical to these atoms. It is an easy mistake to make. If each thing is composed of atoms, why not consider the atom itself as the foundation of a thing's reality? This error was even easier at the beginning of the modern period when scientists such as Newton himself held that atoms were indestructible, eternal, the rock-bottom foundation of the universe. Eventually people came to think that to be a thing meant to be an aggregate of atoms, nothing more, nothing less.

To throw reductionistic materialism into doubt is going to be an upsetting experience for industrial society. I sometimes think the effects on contemporary culture will be similar to those experienced in an earlier period of human history when the idea of the divine rights of kings was thrown into question. People for centuries, even for millennia, had taken as obvious the right of the king's family to rule. Kings were thought to be either divine, as in classical Egypt, or directly descended from divinity, as in ancient India, or divinely ordained, as in medieval Europe.

Suddenly a new idea appeared suggesting that kings were neither divine nor divinely ordained to rule, and that the real seat of political authority rested not with some genetically determined subset of humanity but with the entire people. Thus began the change in consciousness that led to the democratic revolutions that are transforming the world.

I realize that, in comparing our reductionistic materialism with the divine rights of kings, I am comparing metaphysics with political philosophy and this may, at first glance, seem inappropriate. But the political implications of reductionistic materialism are real enough. To appreciate them we need only note the connection between our conviction that material things are the foundation of reality and our devotion to consumerism.

If material stuff is understood to be the very foundation of being, we are quite naturally going to devote our lives and our education to the task of acquiring such stuff, for humans have an innate tropism for being. We move naturally toward that which we are convinced has greater being and value. Just as an earlier age devoted itself to serving the dictates of kings in order to become directly involved with the really real, so too does our age dedicate itself to acquiring commodities in order to enter the wonderworld promised by advertisers. To now suggest that material things are not the only foundational reality in the universe throws some doubt on one of the philosophical justifications of consumerism. And to begin doubting the unquestioned foundations of society's convictions is a dangerously creative and possibly destructive activity, as most monarchs, had they survived, would no doubt agree.

The revelation coming out of quantum physics is that the ground of being is an empty fullness, a fecund nothingness. Even though this realm may be difficult to understand or even to visualize, we can even so draw an elementary conclusion. The base of reality is not inert. The base of the universe is not a bottom-of-the-barrel thing. The base of the universe seethes with such creativity that some physicists refer to the foundation as "space-time foam." In order to integrate this scientific discovery into our daily lives, we need to examine something ordinary from the perspective of quantum field theory. For instance, moonlight. How does the discovery of quantum fields alter our experience of moonlight? We will explore this in detail in the next chapter.

15
All-Nourishing Abyss

The true significance of the discovery of the quantum field is the new understanding it provides concerning the reality of the *nonvisible*. I say nonvisible rather than invisible, for many things are "invisible" to us and yet are capable of being seen. Individual atoms are too small for the unassisted human eye to detect, but atoms can be seen if they are magnified sufficiently. The nonvisible, on the other hand, is that which can never be seen, because it is neither a material thing nor an energy constellation. In addition, the nonvisible world's nature differs so radically from the material world that it cannot even be pictured. It is both nonvisible and *nonvisualizable*. Even so, it is profoundly real and profoundly powerful. Appropriation of the new cosmology requires recognition of the reality and power of the nonvisible and nonmaterial realm.

In contemporary physics, the nonvisible realm is not pictured or given any sort of geometric form. It is rather depicted mathematically and is referred to with such words as "quantum fields," "quantum potential," "false vacuum," and "possibility waves." For simplicity, I want to refer to this nonmaterial realm with a single phrase, and there are many possibilities to choose from.

We could simply use one of the phrases from physics, such as the "universal wave function." But the drawbacks to this are twofold. First is the matter of misusing the languages of science. Science is not the same as cosmology, even when a cosmology is deeply informed by science. Cosmology is the story of the birth, development, and destiny of the universe, told with the aim of assisting humans in their task of identifying their roles within the great drama. Science, however, is focused on obtaining a detailed understanding of the physical processes of the universe. Languages created for science were not created to work for cosmology, and to burden them with this larger role would undoubtedly lead to undesirable ambiguities.

The second drawback to taking over science's languages for cosmological purposes is the unnecessary baggage of modern science's materialistic, mechanistic, and reductionistic bias. Even though scientific exploration colored by this bias did result in the discovery of the realm of nonmaterial power, the language of modern science will continue to be burdened by its history. To take over phrases directly from science is to risk confining the human imagination in the narrow corridors of the industrial consciousness of the last couple of centuries.

An equally attractive way of identifying the ground of the universe would be to take not science's language but theology's. Certainly it is true that humans within classical traditions have reflected upon generative possibility for millennia now, and though this meditation was based on modes of inquiry different from those of modern science, it brought forth insights of profound significance in the quest for understanding. Instead of speaking of the particles as foaming forth from the universal wave function or the quantum field, theologians would speak of the generative powers of the Logos, or God.

As in the case of using science's words, theological language is problematic for contemporary cosmology. Theology is the rational inquiry into the nature of God and of humanity's relationship with God. Theological terms of discourse were not invented to tell the story of the universe, and to force theology's terminology into the service of cosmology would almost certainly create a lot of unnecessary confusion.

Another serious difficulty with utilizing theology's terms is the residue laced into modern theology. During the modern period much of theology focused on the unique aspects of the human-divine relationship, and this tended to give theology a subtle and sometimes outright bias against nonhuman nature. The great news of our time is the evolutionary story in which we come to realize that we humans are all embedded in a living, developing universe, and that we are therefore cousins to everything else in the universe. To employ theological language emphasizing our separateness from the universe is to burden our endeavor with unnecessary baggage.

Cosmology as an ancient wisdom tradition draws from science, theology, art, poetry, and philosophy, but is, strictly speaking, its own distinct tradition. Its terminology does not eschew scientific or theological terms altogether, but generally seeks to make use of language arising out of our experience of living within an unfolding cosmos.

I use "all-nourishing abyss" as a way of pointing to this mystery at the base of being. One advantage of this designation is its dual emphasis: the universe's generative potentiality is indicated with the phrase "all-nourishing," but the universe's power of infinite absorption is indicated with "abyss."

The universe emerges out of the all-nourishing abyss not only fourteen billion years ago but in every moment. At every instant protons and antiprotons are flashing out of, and are as suddenly absorbed back into, the all-nourishing abyss. The all-nourishing abyss is thus not a thing, or a collection of things, or even, strictly speaking, a physical place, but rather a power that gives birth and that absorbs existence at a thing's annihilation.

The foundational reality of the universe is this unseen ocean of potentiality. If all the individual things of the universe were to evaporate, one would be left with an infinity of pure generative power.

Each particular thing is directly and essentially grounded in the all-nourishing abyss. Though we think of our bodies as dense and completely filling up the space they occupy, careful investigation of matter has shown that this is not the case. The volume of elementary particles is extremely small when compared to the volume of the atoms that they form. Thus, the essential nature of any atom is less material than it is "empty space." From this perspective we can begin to see that the root foundation of any thing or any being is not the matter out of which it is composed so much as the matter together with the power that gives rise to the matter.

The all-nourishing abyss is acting ceaselessly throughout the universe. It is not possible to find any place in the universe that is outside this activity. Even in the darkest regions of the universe, even in the void between the superclusters, even in the gaps between the synapses of the neurons in the brain, there occurs an incessant foaming, a flashing flame, a shining-forth-from and a dissolving-back-into.

The importance of the cosmological tradition is its power to awaken those deep convictions necessary for wisdom. Knowledge of the all-nourishing abyss is the beginning of a process that reaches its fulfillment in direct experience. We think long and hard about such matters as a way of preparing ourselves for tasting and feeling the depths of a reality that has always been present and yet so subtle it escaped us.

It may be that in the new millennium spiritual orientations will be awakened and established within the young, primarily by meaningful encounters with the mysteries of the universe. The task of education then will focus on learning how to "read" the universe so that one might enter and inhabit the universe as a communion event.

Let us turn now to the question of how our experience of moonlight will change. I'd like simply to consider the Moon at night and to indicate how, within the new omnicentric cosmology, the Moon can become an activator of a new dimension of consciousness.

Before we had an understanding of the quantum nature of the universe we could so easily think of the Moon as an astronomical object. Its light was thought of as light from the Sun that had been reflected our way. And of course there's some truth here, for if the Sun were suddenly to go dark then the Moon too would go dark. But there is another and more subtle quantum sense in which the Moon is not just an object and its light is not just reflected from the Sun.

Newton and others early in the modern period regarded the Moon as a conglomeration of stable, unchanging atoms. With such a conception it is easy to hold that the Moon simply forms a wall off of which the light from the Sun bounces. But when we examine the physical processes of "light," "atoms," and "bounce," we find a much more complex and even astounding dynamic.

First, the elementary particles and atoms are not permanently existing objects but are events that are vibrating at extremely rapid rates. Even the word "vibrate" is not exact, for it connotes a solid object that moves rapidly back and forth in space. This gives a false image of the quantum realm, for it is not the case that particles are moving back and forth in space. Rather, as scientists discovered in the twentieth century, particles exist in one location and then exist in another location *without traversing the space in between*. So, as bewildering as it might sound to us, it is more accurate scientifically to say that the particles and atoms are flashing into existence, surging into existence, and then just as suddenly they are dissolving from their place to surge forth in a nearby location, with all this happening so rapidly that the unassisted human eye cannot catch the movement.

The Moon is not a dead object. The Moon is an ongoing scintillating event.

Second, it is false to think of photons as "bouncing" the way a ball bounces when thrown against a wall. Instead, the photons from the Sun "interact" with the particles of the Moon. As with every interaction at the quantum level of reality, this interaction begins with the annihilation of the particles as they are absorbed into the all-nourishing abyss and is followed by the creation of a new set of particles. If this new set contains any photons, these photons are *new*. They did not exist in the previous instant. They came forth out of the annihilating event of the interaction.

Thus, it is not true to say that the photons of light arriving here from the Moon have just been bounced from the Sun. Moonlight comes from the Moon. Moonlight is *created* by the Moon.

In the twenty-first century, young people educated in the new cosmology will experience the Moon not as a frozen lump but as an event that trembles into existence each moment. Moonlight will be understood as *expressive* of the Moon's reality. The Moon will be seen as a creative source, an origin of the universe, a geyser that sprays moonlight into the night sky.

Through such encounters we learn that the universe is not a collection of dead objects but a community of cosmos-creating subjects.

When children learn of the universe's birth, they ask, "What was before?" These minds of ours, emerging fourteen billion years after the great flaring forth; these minds of ours, woven tapestries of the same primal particles emerging in the beginning; these minds of ours insist upon knowing what is at their own base. We wish to know the nature of the reality from which we arose, for then we will know our own deepest nature.

Humans of every culture have contemplated this mystery, and we in the twenty-first century now enter the cosmological lineage with our own contribution. We too have contacted, in our own unique way, the Great Power that gave birth to the universe fourteen billion years ago and that continues to give birth in every interaction throughout the universe today. From our own fresh empirical-mathematical contemplation, we have identified a nonmaterial realm suffusing the microcosm of every being in the universe. That which gave birth to the universe is giving birth in this moment as well. Although our understanding is very young, and thus inadequate in many ways, what we have discovered is already deeply stirring.

Quantum field theory identified the domain of cosmic birth. We now know we are not just the atoms of our bodies, for we are as well the realm out of which these atoms arise. We are led inexorably to reflect upon the thrilling and unnerving fact that the power that gave birth to the universe suffuses our flesh and blood. Is that the best image for what it means to be human? Are we then that unique animal that has become aware that it lives in the kingdom where the dream of the universe becomes reality?

16

Einstein's Awakening

After all these theoretical discussions on the large-scale structures of the universe and the origin of matter, I want now to turn to something concrete, to a person, to a specific moment in time. My hope is that if we can understand these ideas as they pertain to an actual human, we will have a better sense of how they shed light on our own lives.

So we turn one last time to Albert Einstein. It is not Einstein the person that I am primarily interested in; it is Einstein as an image of our intimate connection to the creativity of the evolving universe. In order to reflect further on this I want to return to that pivotal night when Einstein was hunched over his equations in his second-story Berlin apartment.

So there he sits, this human, with his frame descended from the primates and now held aloft twenty inches by rented furniture. Even if no actual drums are playing as Einstein contemplates the structure of the universe, certainly from our later understanding of the significance of this moment we can imagine that in the dark night there thunders a kind of silent music in celebration of what is taking place.

A strange moment certainly, and yet so much that is familiar too. His pipe leaning on its side, forgotten, the ashes dead for an hour now. The room heavy with the sweet, sharp smell of the old smoke. Outside, raining still, the few people on the streets below hurrying under caps and dark coats. But Einstein hasn't looked out the window all evening, and even if he had, the sensory images would hardly have penetrated his consciousness. Unaware of the rain, or the cold pipe, or the light weight of the pencil in his hand, yet profoundly aware, and very alert, even heavy laden with consciousness, a sort of consciousness that lives best near the edge of the world, a region he seems to have occupied so often.

Years later psychological investigators would question Einstein about his consciousness during such moments of radical creativity, and he stunned them with his reply. They had been curious about Einstein's mathematical orientation. Most mathematical scientists fall into one of two qualitatively distinct mental domains. One is the algebraic, in which an investigator will rely on the formalisms of equations with alphabetic letters and algorithmic rules for transforming one symbol set into another. The other is the geometric, where, instead of using abstract formulas, an investigator relies upon shapes and spatially constructed scenarios. After interviewing a number of world-class mathematical scientists, the investigators had grown accustomed to

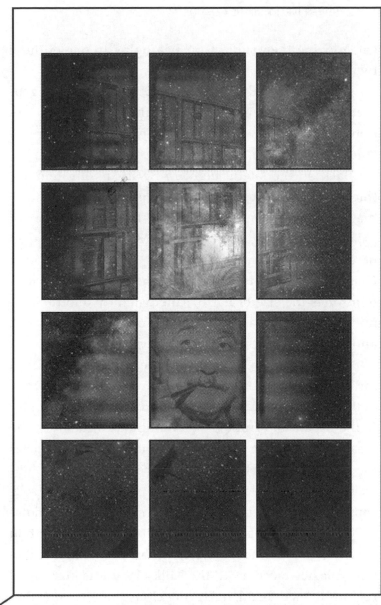

categorizing their subjects as belonging to one of these two domains.

Instead of speaking of algebraic formalisms or geometric intuitions Einstein, after reflecting on the question carefully, answered that his experiences were of "the muscular type."

Back on the fateful night in Berlin, as Einstein sat, thick with awareness, his hands inscribing the mathematical symbols on the page, the Hercules Cluster of galaxies was racing away from the Milky Way at a speed of eighteen thousand miles each second. The Coma Cluster of galaxies too, all its trillions of stars each a million times the size of Earth, sailed silently into the cosmic night. There was no awareness of this on our planet, and there Einstein sat, receptive and waiting.

Fourteen billion years earlier the universe had flared forth with stupendous energy, and in that primordial fire of the beginning each individual point was the still center of the expansion. Through the numinous alchemy of the creativity pervading the cosmos, some of the first particles there at the center baked into a living body called Einstein, who sat meditating, protected from the rains of self-contempt, or financial insecurity, or needless distraction.

Several times each year the Milky Way gives birth to a new star. As Einstein sat there in his room and the distant galaxies raced away, the Milky Way was busy in all regions of its domain, nurturing clouds of elements that sat brooding with the potentiality for star birth. I wish I could write with certainty that simultaneous with Einstein's awakening to the dynamics of the large-scale structure of space-time a star was born in one of the arms of the Milky Way. But even if this simultaneous birth did not take place, it is nevertheless true that in both instances we have a patch of the Milky Way, thick with the fecundity of the galaxy, churning with urgency, approaching a new creation out of the multivalent potentiality of the Milky Way.

Einstein eventually despaired of ever explaining his experience of creativity to others. So many suffered under a distorted understanding. He did not, he told them patiently, simply study data and then look for equations that fit the data. The truth of the matter, so difficult for them to accept, was that he himself relied primarily on imagination.

When Einstein—this piece of the Milky Way—was asked what he sought, he answered: "I want to know how the Old One thinks. The rest is a detail." This creature wearing worn-out shoes, this mustachioed member of the notochord phylum, this living flesh with its creases from a lifetime of laughter, this lumpy concentration of molecules, this soul open to wonder burned to know how the Old One thinks. How the Old One is shaping the great vaults of the heavens. How the Old One is casting a billion stars in their circlings. How the Old One is fastening the baryons together. How the Old One is releasing electromagnetism throughout the cellular membranes.

Chock-full with the very dynamics he was contemplating, Einstein experienced a birth that permeated him whole, his mind, his muscles, his viscera. Effortlessly, and as a form of these very dynamics, he jotted down the field equations. This chunk of the Milky Way jotted down the dynamics of the Milky Way. This region of space-time, rich with the interactions of the universe, jotted down the symbolic form of the interactions of the universe. This fleshy portion of the world transformed its inwardness through graphite to reveal the harmonies at work throughout the fleshy world.

The Indians of South America teach that to become human "one must make room in oneself for the immensities of the universe." Unless we do so, we cannot find our true nature. We will wander in pain and loneliness. We will never learn how the Old One thinks.

Making room for the immensities, Einstein experienced their inrush, when suddenly the Milky Way as Great Self became this Einstein reflecting upon his deepest nature, which is the nature of the galaxy and of the cosmos too. Afterward, when he had calmed down and was attempting to make sense of what had happened, he did distort some of what had emerged. He added a symbol. He changed what he had intuited. In the cultural calm away from the thundering breakthrough he gave in to the habits of his time and place and altered his original equations—a shrinking back that we can reflect on to our benefit.

But in that great moment, in that state of consciousness coming from years of disciplined preparation, *Einstein was not contemplating something apart from himself.* He was absorbed in the experience of the feelings in his body, his viscera, that were caused by the causes permeating the universe. That Great Power that had, there, at the birthplace of the universe, emanated all the energies and galaxies was now bringing forth its own self-portrait in the symbols of Einstein's field equations. Powers that would one day receive such names as "the second law of thermodynamics" or "the strong nuclear interaction"; powers that shaped the Milky Way Galaxy and the mammals; those were at work in that concentrated form of the Milky Way called Einstein, and it was there that this Great Power broke into a new contemplation of its sublime grandeur.

17

The Center of the Cosmos

The universe began as an eruption of space, time, matter, and energy out of an all-nourishing abyss, the hidden heart of universe creativity. The cosmos began as a titanic bestowal, a stupendous quantum of free energy given forth from the bottomless vaults of generosity.

The nature of this original gift goes so far beyond our daily human experiences that we must resort to numbers to approach it. In the first second, the universe is a million times hotter than the center of our Sun today. It is in an extremely compact form. The original matter is a billion times denser than rock. And yet this primordial matter expands more rapidly than the speed of light.

Every place in the universe is at the center of this exploding reality. From our place on Earth today in the midst of the Virgo Supercluster, all of the other superclusters of the universe sail away from us. The same is true for anyone with awareness of the universe from the perspective of the Perseus Supercluster. Each supercluster is at the unmoving center of this cosmic expansion where we have existed from the beginning of time.

When the primordial fireball erupted into being, it was so hot that no structures could exist, but as the expansion continued, and as the temperatures slowly came down, the first assembled beings began to appear. Protons and neutrons joined each other in constructing the simple communities called nuclei. After three hundred thousand years the temperature dropped to six thousand degrees, the same as the surface of our Sun today, and the universe transformed itself from the plasma of elementary particles and simple nuclei into the first atoms of hydrogen, helium, and lithium. This same spectacular transformation continued into the future, when these atoms combined to form the galaxies, then the molecules and cells, and then humans and the Mississippi River.

To enter the omnicentric unfolding universe is to taste the joy of radical relational mutuality, for we know that the atoms of our body could just as easily have found themselves within a giant sequoia. We could have been a migrating pelican. Or an asteroid. Or molten lava, or a woman or a man, or a cumulus cloud.

Scientific observation and reasoning has led us to these insights concerning the birth and development of the universe. These discoveries are as great as any throughout the history of humanity. But here, as we conclude our discussion, I think it is important to remind ourselves that the heart of the cosmos is not "mathematical science," nor is it "owned" by science. The heart of the cosmos is at work in each event in the cosmos. Science is one of the careful and detailed methods by which the human mind comes to grasp the fact of the universe's beginning, but the actual origin is not a scientific idea. The actual origin of the universe is where we live our lives. It is that place where the great birth happened at the beginning of time and is happening now in the upwelling of river and star and feeling. The person who learns she is at the origin of the universe is herself an origin of the universe. Our awareness, like our atoms, is rooted in the originating activity. We are, instant by instant, arising together out of the hidden heart of the cosmos.

Index

advertising industry, 103
  children as shaped by, 12, 13, 17
  consumerism as the dominant
    world faith, 15, 16
  dissatisfaction and craving,
    generating, 14
all-nourishing abyss, 108–9, 111,
  120
Andromeda Galaxy
  as a chance creation, 94
  children, introducing to the
    light of, 53–55
  photons of light arriving to
    earth from, 60
  Virgo Supercluster, as part of,
    70
atoms, 122
  atomic theory of matter, 102
  in classical Greek understand-
    ing, 101
  empty space as essential nature
    of, 108
  hydrogen atoms, Sun formed
    by, 36
  instability in the first instants
    of time, 90–91
  magnification required to view,
    105
  in modern cosmology, 85–86,
    88–89
  quantum field and, 99, 112
  relational mutuality of, 121
  as surging in and out of
    existence, 110–11

Berry, Thomas, xiii, xv, 30
birthplace of the universe, 22
  discovery of as a learning
    event, 1, 3, 61, 63
  field equations of Einstein as
    revealing, 64–68, 119
  as fourteen billion light-years
    ago, 57, 72, 77
  Hubble, Edwin, role in discovery
    of, 57–58
  as most significant discovery of
    the 20th century, 2, 40
  in mythical and classical
    consciousness, 70
  new cosmological understand-
    ings, 73, 98

clusters, 109
  Hercules Cluster, 79, 116
  as moving apart from each
    other, 81
  as moving away from earth, 69,
    74
  vacuum as the region between
    superclusters, 99
  Virgo Supercluster, 55–56, 58,
    70, 75, 83, 120
consciousness, 103
  classical consciousness, 34, 70,
    72
  cosmovisions of early humans,
    49
  of current generation, 61
  of Einstein, 114, 118

industrial consciousness, 9, 29, 31, 101, 106
the moon, activating a new dimension of, 109
new cosmology, consciousness transformed through, 40
Newtonian consciousness, 77
ordinary consciousness, moving from, 21
of primates, 45, 86
consumerism and the consumer society, 13–17, 30, 93, 103
Copernicus, Nicolaus, 18–20, 32–33, 74–75, 76
cosmology
  advertising as shaping personal cosmologies, 15–16
  Copernicus, cosmological exploration of, 76
  cosmological education, 33, 52
  cosmological relationships, developing, 49
  cosmological wonderment, early expressions of, 7–8
  as its own distinct tradition, 107
  !Kung cosmology, 88
  lack of cosmological awareness, 11, 29–30, 53
  language of science as insufficient for, 106
  Newtonian cosmology, 65, 78
  omnicentric cosmology, 84–85, 109
  pre-Einsteinian cosmologies, 18, 65
  raisin loaf imagery, 80
  the Sun and, 34–36, 38
  See also new cosmology

Democritus, 101
Descartes, René, 93
divine rights of kings, 102–3

Earth, 49
  as center of the universe, 18–19

direct sensation of earth's turning, 24–25, 28
earth-time, sense of, 95
gravity and, 26–27
Milky Way, relationship with, 44–45, 48
religion, role of Earth in, 10
as revolving around the Sun, 39, 46, 55, 58, 74–75
size of, 33
split-modern sense of, 21–22
stars, experiencing as below the earth, 46–47
Sun, receiving vitality from, 35, 36, 38
Virgo Supercluster, as part of, 55, 58, 83, 120
Earth Community, 3, 51
education, 11
  cosmological education, 31, 33, 79–80, 109, 111
  Ecozoic education, transitioning into, 51
  moral education, 15–16, 39
  Newtonian foundation of educational systems, 77
  science education as lacking, 10
  transformation of subjectivity as goal of, 22
Einstein, Albert
  altering of troublesome data, 58, 66–67, 76, 118
  difficulties accepting theory, 5–6, 68, 75, 79
  night of discovery, re-imagining, 64–66, 113–19
  on the size of the universe, 57, 83
  special theory of relativity, 65, 94–97

field equations
  birthplace of the universe, revealing, 64–68, 119
  of Einstein, 97, 117–18

fixity of the galaxies, prior supposition of, 75–76
omnicentric universe, revealing, 84
Friedmann, Alexander, 67–68

galaxies. *See* Local Group of galaxies; Milky Way galaxy
Galileo, 33, 66, 76
General Theory of Relativity, 57, 65
Greeks, ancient, 34, 101
Grim, John, xiii, xv

Hercules Cluster, 79, 116
Hubble, Edwin, 57, 64
    Einstein, inviting to Mount Palomar, 68
    expansion of the galaxies, discovering, 74, 77, 83
    as publishing data without interpretation, 58, 76

Journey of the Universe project, xiii
Jupiter, 20, 24, 48

Kaang, role in !Kung cosmology, 85, 86, 88
Kant, Immanuel, 62

Laudato Si' encyclical, xiii
Lemaître, Georges, 69, 71–72, 83
light, types of
    from the Andromeda Galaxy, 53–54, 60
    from the birth of the universe, 77, 78, 82, 83
    moonlight, 62, 63, 109–10, 111
    starlight, 42, 44
    sunlight, 33, 36
    See also photons
light-year, defining, 52
Local Group of galaxies, 55–56, 58, 69

Magellanic Clouds, 55, 70

mammals, eyes evolving to front of face, 22–23
materialism, 28
    of advertising culture, 17
    crass materialism of the modern period, 15, 35
    materialistic bias of modern science, 106
    reductionist materialism, 101, 102–3
mathematics, 43, 60
    atoms, mathematical laws as controlling, 88, 91
    birthplace of the universe, calculating, 70
    cosmological constant as a mathematical term, 67
    mathematical theories, scientists not projecting, 58
    non-visible realm as depicted mathematically, 105
mental domains, types of, 114–16
Milky Way Galaxy, 75
    Andromeda Galaxy and, 53–54
    conscious experience of, 42
    contemplation of, 43–48, 51–52
    Einstein as a piece of, 117–19
    as expanding, 69
    in Local Group system, 55, 58
    new stars, creation of, 97, 116–17
moonlight, 62, 63, 109–10, 111
myths and mythical consciousness, 34, 67, 70, 72

Neolithic era, 21, 70
new cosmology, 90
    consciousness as transformed by, 40
    cultural support as lacking for, 28
    emotional reactions to fundamental cosmological changes, 93
    fear and joy, evoking, 31, 98–99

moon, enhanced understanding of, 111
non-visible and non-material realm, recognizing, 105
religion of consumerism, rejecting, 17
scientific discoveries, role in, 3
Newton, Isaac, 33
on atoms as the foundation of the universe, 88, 102
Einstein as shattering the Newtonian worldview, 65
Newtonian consciousness, insufficiency of, 77
Newtonian cosmology, 78
Newtonian understanding, leaving behind, 80
on space as empty and fixed, 66, 79, 83, 94–95, 99, 100
stability of the Moon, belief in, 110
theory of absolute space and time, 96
night
inversion of the night sky, imagining, 46–47
sacred nature of, 42, 62–63
non-visible realm, 105–6

Oedipus Rex, split life in, 50–51
Old One, Einstein referencing, 17
omnicentricity, 84, 93, 98
Einstein, initial reaction to, 79
moon, role in omnicentric cosmology, 109
philosophical doctrine of, 85, 86
psychological obstacles toward experiencing, 94
raisin loaf model, 80
relational mutuality and, 121

Palomar, Mount, 68
Penzias, Arno, 72, 77, 82–83
photons, 58
ancient nature of, 52–53, 54

from Andromeda Galaxy, 60
dim light of, 1
as moonlight, 111
release at birth of the universe, 72, 73, 82
as sunlight, 35
primates and primal perception, 21, 23, 45–46, 49, 56, 86
psychedelics, 29–30, 31

quantum philosophy
ground of being, quantum physics on, 103–4
the moon, quantum sense of, 110
quantum field theory, 105, 107, 112
quantum interactions in the all-nourishing abyss, 111
quantum vacuum, particles emerging in, 99–100

reductionist materialism, 101, 102–3
Relativity, Theory of
general theory of relativity, 57, 65
special theory of relativity, 65, 94–97
Rogers Centre, 41

Sagittarius constellation, 51, 52
science, 30
ancient traditions, integrating with, 2–3
atomic theory of matter as robust, 102
change of perception and, 22
as a collective enterprise, 67
contemporary science and Copernicus, 25, 32–33
cosmology and, 29, 106–7
counterintuitive nature of scientific discoveries, 21
hypotheses, constantly revising, 71

as a method of understanding the universe, 121–22

modern science, early views of, 88–89

religion, as divided from, 10–11

scientific consciousness on birth of the universe, 72

sense of superiority arising from, 43

Special Theory of Relativity, extensive testing of, 95

speculative cosmology as an extension of, 84

SkyDome, 41, 43

Slipher, Vesto, 57, 64

Sophocles, 50

Soviet Union, indoctrination practices of, 12–13

Special Theory of Relativity, 65, 94–97

split life as a modern condition, 22, 50–51

Sun

centrality of, 18–20, 21, 32–33, 76

Earth as revolving around, 39, 46, 55, 58, 74–75

gravitational pull of, 47

Milky Way, preventing view of, 45

moonlight and, 110, 111

sacrifice of, 34–35, 38

size of, 26, 33, 48

solar system, contemplating, 24–28

sunlight, 33, 35, 36

temperature of, 120, 121

theological terms, as problematic for cosmology, 106–8

time

Newtonian sense of time as universal, 94–95, 96

space and time, simultaneous emergence of, 78

space-time foam, 104

tools, early use of, 2, 20, 54, 61

Tucker, Mary Evelyn, xiii, xv

universal wave function, 106, 107

universe

as the all-nourishing abyss, 108–9, 111, 120

fecund emptiness of, 100, 103–4

focus of universe on its parts, 93–94

modern mechanical view, 88–89

order of, leading to individual empowerment, 96–97

primordial desire of, 90–91

theological terminology as inadequate to describe, 107

See also birthplace of the universe

vacuum. See quantum philosophy

Venus, 24–25, 26

Virgo Supercluster, 55–56, 58, 70, 75, 83, 120

Wilson, Robert, 72, 77, 82–83